MARGARET M. JOHNSON'S

 *in* IRELAND

PRAISE FOR *TEATIME IN IRELAND*

"Pull up a chair, pour yourself a steaming cup of your favorite tea, and then settle in for a feast for the taste buds as well as the eyes. From custards to creams, cakes to éclairs, and dainty sandwiches to tartines, Margaret Johnson's latest cookbook is an encyclopedic, lavishly illustrated journey through the celebrated custom of teatime in Ireland. Learn the fascinating history behind Ireland's iconic beverage, the time-honored repast that complements it, and learn about the shops, hotels, and castles that do it best. *Teatime in Ireland* is essential reading and a valuable addition to your cookbook collection."

—JEFF MEADE,
Editor, irishphiladelphia.com

"*Teatime in Ireland* is Margaret Johnson's most glorious book yet. Full of rich history and traditional sayings, every page will make you want to put on a kettle of water to make a rich, soul-satisfying brew. Visit legendary tea spots through her pages or create your own specialties for friends and family. There is absolutely no better way to create a bit of peace and joy in your day."

—ROSEANN TULLY,
CEO & Founder, *Intermezzo* Magazine

"Margaret Johnson's *Teatime in Ireland* brings us the best of Irish cooking with a visual presentation of Ireland that creates a longing for home. And this latest volume, like its predecessors, is literate and entertaining, as well as informative and practical."

—PETER MCDERMOTT,
Arts Editor, *Irish Echo* Newspaper

"With her latest book, *Teatime in Ireland,* Margaret Johnson proves again to be one of Irish gastronomy's most fervent, accomplished, and artful ambassadors. She presents scores of recipes—and stories—each practically arranged, sourced, and delicious, along with lustrous photos that literally beckon the appetite. For this reader, at least, the book now stands as the definitive guide to the rich culture of Irish tea rooms. Indeed, as the book highlights, what other ritual could inspire its devotees to their cupán tea at Dublin's Shelbourne Hotel on Easter Monday 1916, as the bullets flew in and around them!"

—GERRY REGAN,
Editorial Director, thewildgeese.irish Social Network

MRS. WHITE'S AFTERNOON TEA, DROMOLAND CASTLE, Dromoland Castle

THE CONNAGHT ROOM, ASHFORD CASTLE, Ashford Castle

Margaret M. Johnson

DEDICATION

For my parents and grandparents
—the McGlews, Barrys, O'Sullivans, and Crowleys—
thanks for my Irish heritage.

Piotr Skubisz | *Dreamstime.com*

Teatime in Ireland

© 2019 by Margaret M. Johnson
All Rights Reserved

ISBN: 978-1-62020-975-2
E-ISBN: 978-1-88989-314-3

Cover photos: (Clockwise, from top left) TEA AT THE SHELBOURNE, Shelbourne Hotel; BATTENBERG CAKE, Andrew Norton | Dreamstime.com; BUNRATTY FOLK PARK, Margaret M. Johnson; ANTIQUE TEA CUPS, Margaret M. Johnson; CRANBERRY-GINGER DROP SCONES Creantive | Dreamstime.com

Back cover photo: Jessica Guadagno

Cover design & page layout by Hannah Nichols
Ebook conversion by Anna Riebe Raats

AMBASSADOR INTERNATIONAL
Emerald House
411 University Ridge, Suite B14
Greenville, SC 29601, USA
www.ambassador-international.com

AMBASSADOR BOOKS
The Mount
2 Woodstock Link
Belfast, BT6 8DD, Northern Ireland, UK
www.ambassadormedia.co.uk

The colophon is a trademark of Ambassador

MARGARET M. JOHNSON'S

Teatime in IRELAND

AMBASSADOR INTERNATIONAL
GREENVILLE, SOUTH CAROLINA & BELFAST, NORTHERN IRELAND
www.ambassador-international.com

CONTENTS

KERRY COTTAGE, Margaret M. Johnson

INTRODUCTION

May you always have walls for the winds,
a roof for the rain, tea beside the fire,
laughter to cheer you, those you love near you,
and all your heart might desire.

AN IRISH BLESSING

You might say that in Ireland all roads lead to tea. From breakfast and lunch breaks to weddings and wakes, *cupán tea* is always a welcome guest. Irish tea is far more than just a hot drink to go with a scone and jam: it's an important custom that serves as a symbol of hospitality, friendship, and pleasure. Some say the Irish people have a relationship with tea that "transcends the ordinary"—hyperbole, perhaps, but given that the average person in Ireland drinks four to six cups of tea a day, perhaps not!

Teatime in Ireland is actually my favorite time of day. I enjoyed my first official cup at my cousin Kit's cottage in County Kerry during my first visit there 35 years ago. Within minutes of our meeting, the kettle was on, the teacups were out, and the milk and sugar appeared. A box of Jacob's Rich Tea biscuits quickly followed, and Chocolate Kimberley biscuits for my children arrived on a small plate. Our relationship was ceremoniously underway.

For years, I had known Kit only as "my Irish cousin": a distant relative twice, maybe even three times removed whom I'd never met. Christmas cards were exchanged over the years like pen pals, but this in-person visit with cup in hand closed the gap between cousins from across the pond. Funny enough, we couldn't actually connect the dots in our ancestry chain—she was an O'Sullivan who dropped the "O" while my grandmother was an O'Sullivan who kept the "O"—but none of that really mattered. We sipped our tea and sealed the deal.

We repeated this ritual each time I visited Ireland, usually once a year, but later I supplied the sweets. I bought cookie "collections" in fancy tins with photos of local scenes like Moll's Gap or Ross Castle at tourist shops in Killarney. Or I bought treats from Jam, a local bakery known for its heavenly scones and fruity crumbles. Teatime in Ireland was terrific.

The *cuppa* with my cousin was just the beginning of other wonderful teatime experiences, especially afternoon tea—the elegant three-course affair where tea is the main attraction and delicacies like dainty sandwiches, flaky scones, and luscious pastries act in supporting roles. Introduced in England in the mid-1840s, the mini-meal grew in popularity there and eventually spread to Ireland. I have to admit I fell under its spell when a friend first suggested we meet in Dublin and have tea at The Shelbourne, one of Ireland's most legendary hotels. Without a tea biscuit or Kimberley in sight, we settled into a tea stand laden with traditional tea sandwiches—cucumber, smoked salmon, and creamy egg salad; plain and fruity scones with clotted cream, lemon curd, and strawberry jam; elegant tartlets, cream-filled éclairs, and macarons. The tea selection ranged from aromatic Darjeeling to citrus-scented Earl Grey and exotic Lapsang Souchong. Heaven!

I was smitten, to say the least, and in *Teatime in Ireland* I'll share some of my most memorable tea experiences along with recipes that you'll be excited to offer guests at your next tea. *Teatime in Ireland* will transport you to legendary hotel tea spots like Ashford Castle, Adare Manor, The Merrion Hotel, and Dromoland Castle, and to smaller venues like Cupán Tea in Galway and Castlewood House in Dingle; recipes from Irish home cooks join the mix.

Be prepared to wow your guests by serving specialties like Smoked Salmon on Guinness Treacle Bread, Raspberry Crumble Tray Bake, Battenberg Cake, and Bakewell Tarts. Perfect for armchair travelers, food tourists, and anyone with a thirst for the Emerald Isle, *Teatime in Ireland* will provide both a delicious culinary and cultural experience and offer a treasure trove of recipes from homespun tea loaves to elegant cakes and tarts—perfect for hosting your own special occasion afternoon tea. *Bain taitneamh as do bhéile . . . Bon appétit!*

CHAPTER ONE

A Little History of Tea

If you are cold, tea will warm you; if you are too heated, it will cool you;
if you are depressed it will cheer you; if you are excited, it will calm you.
Thank God for tea! What would the world do without tea!
I am glad I was not born before tea.

WILLIAM GLADSTONE, BRITISH PRIME MINISTER

THE story of tea began in China; one early reference to it dates back to 2737 B.C. According to legend, a Chinese emperor named Shen Nung sat under a tree as he boiled water for drinking. Some leaves from the *Camellia sinensis* tree fell into the boiling water and gave the emperor his first cup of what we now call "tea." Whether the story is true or not, tea drinking was established in China many centuries before it made its way to the West.

The first teas grown for export were sent to Britain from China about 300 years ago. Tea arrived in Ireland in the early 1830s thanks to the Bewley's, Samuel and his son Charles, who dared to break the East India Company's monopoly by importing 2,099 chests of tea on board the clipper ship *The Hellas*, the first ship chartered directly from Canton to Dublin. At the time, Ireland had yet to develop its famous thirst for tea, so the stakes were high if the tea could not be sold. Thankfully, the venture turned out to be more successful than either could possibly have imagined, changing the taste of a nation and making Bewley's a household name in Ireland. Bewley's was officially founded in 1840 as the China Tea Company and expanded into the coffee business and the operation of coffee shops, most notably the legendary Oriental Café, which opened in 1927 on Dublin's Grafton Street.

In 1901, James J. Barry founded Barry's Tea and began selling it from the family's shop on Prince's Street in Cork. From the beginning, quality was at the heart of the Barry family business, and in 1934 his son Anthony Barry was awarded the Empire Cup for tea blending, confirming his expertise in the tea trade. Until the 1960s, Barry's teas were sourced mostly from India and Sri Lanka and were sold mainly from the Prince's Street location. But when their blends grew in popularity, they widened their business and began selling their teas to other shops in Cork,

Michael Arnaud
Dreamstime.com

Awarded the Empire Cup for Tea Blending
Grocers Exhibition London 1934.

BARRY'S
TEA

as well
known as
Shandon!

Barry's Tea

eventually expanding into the suburbs and then out to the rest of Ireland.

In 1902, the Lyons family started their Irish tea business at High Street in Dublin, near Christchurch Cathedral, later moving to premises on Marlborough Street behind the old Gresham hotel. These three brands are the most popular in Ireland today.

During the 1930s, all tea imported into Ireland came from the world-famous London Tea Auction, and the majority of tea produced in the world then, apart from China and Japan, was shipped to London and sold worldwide through the auction. Most of the tea consumed in Ireland was from Ceylon (now Sri Lanka) and Assam, a tropical region nestled in the foothills of the Himalayan Mountains in the northeast corner of India, and all of the tea was purchased through the London Auction and shipped from the UK to Dublin. Ireland always bought the best teas possible to satisfy its appetite for quality tea, a factor that stands true to today where the overall standard of tea sold in Ireland is exceptionally high.

When World War II broke out, however, and Germany started its attacks on Allied convoys heading across the North Atlantic, the British Government requested the use of three deep seaports on the south and west coasts of Ireland. Because Ireland was a neutral country, the government refused. England immediately retaliated, severely reducing the amount of tea (and coal) that could be exported to Ireland. This led to a significant hardship for the Irish, so much so the government decided they would never again be beholden to the United Kingdom for tea (or coal), both essential items. After the war, the Irish Government set up a tea company called Irish Tea Importers Ltd. with the sole responsibility for sourcing tea directly from the country of origin, bypassing the London Tea Auction.

The company established direct contact with India and arranged to purchase Indian tea for shipment directly to Ireland. As a result, every tea company in Ireland had to purchase its tea directly from Irish Tea Importers Ltd. and each one had to become a shareholder. Regardless of company size, they were allowed to purchase equal quantities of only three different tea standards: good quality, medium quality, and lower- medium quality teas. This continued into the mid-1960s.

During this time, John A. FitzPatrick, a shipping clerk with Irish Tea Importers, travelled to Uganda when he learned that East African countries were producing a lovely, bright, golden colored tea using a new production method called C.T.C. (cut, tear, and curl) as opposed to orthodox manufacture where the leaf is rolled after withering it. He also found that Ugandan teas were made year-round while Indian tea was made for only about four months of the year. With Africa being that much closer to Ireland, and tea being made all year, he realized he could get fresher teas delivered to Ireland more quickly and on a year-round basis. In 1962, he established John A. FitzPatrick & Co Ltd. to import tea directly to Ireland.

FitzPatrick faced opposition, however, because Irish customers were used to the large, black, orthodox leaf compared to the brown, small, round C.T.C. type tea from East Africa. To convince them, he brought tea samples to customers directly, pointing out the considerable savings in not having to hold tea stock all year, the freshness of the new tea, and the beautiful bright golden color it produces. He got his big breakthrough when he visited a small tea wholesaler in Prince's Street, Cork, and found that owner Peter Barry loved the idea of this beautiful golden tea from Africa; Barry bought his first consignment.

From the mid-1960s, two things changed the Irish tea market: African C.T.C. leaf was introduced, and consumers gradually changed to using tea bags. More and more teas were imported from East Africa—mainly Kenya, Uganda, and Rwanda—and less from countries like Sri Lanka and Indonesia. The style of tea also changed: blends that were traditionally Indian, Sri Lankan, and Indonesian orthodox teas changed to become blends of Indian and East African C.T.C. teas. Less and less orthodox tea was imported, primarily because smaller grain C.T.C. teas could easily be packed into tea bags. From the 1970s until today, this style of tea accounts for about 99% of the total Irish tea market, and tea bags account for approximately 98% of the market share.

In a span of less than 60 years, the Irish tea market changed dramatically, except for one thing: the love the Irish have for their tea and the quality of that tea. Some studies claim they drink an average of four cups a day making them one of the biggest consumers of tea in the world. The Irish are noted for drinking their tea strong and with lots of milk. Traditionally, milk was poured into teacups first to prevent the hot tea from cracking fine china cups, but what started as a practical method continues today; in fact, tea aficionados have determined that pouring milk into hot tea actually alters its flavor. Sometimes as much as a third of the cup is filled with milk, depending on the tea drinkers' color preference.

A TEA PRIMER

Tea is now grown in nearly fifty countries worldwide from Argentina and Brazil to Mozambique and Kenya. The tea bush thrives in mountainous regions bordering the tropics and can grow at heights of up to 7,000 feet above sea level. Black tea is the world's most common variety, is full-bodied, and has the strongest taste. India, particularly its Assam region, is the world's largest producer and exporter of tea. **Assam** teas are robust with a smooth malty taste. **Darjeeling**, with tea gardens in the foothills of the Himalayas, produces smaller crops of excellent quality and is an ideal complement to dinner or for afternoon tea. Darjeeling is often referred to as "the Champagne of teas" because of its quality and unique "Muscatel" wine flavor.

Ceylon, now Sri Lanka, produces tea still referred to as **Ceylon**. The best quality teas are "high grown" on slopes above 4,000 feet. Ceylon teas are strong but delicate, with a slight bitterness. Kenya now grows some of the very best tea in the world, some grown at nearly 7,000 feet above sea level. These teas are brightly colored with a delicious aroma. China remains famous for its distinctive black, green, and oolong teas. **Lapsang Souchong** has a distinctive smoky taste acquired through drying over pine wood fires. **Keemun**, the traditional tea of old Imperial China, is known for its orchid aroma and brilliant red liquor. It's frequently used as the base for scented blends, the most popular of which is **Earl Grey**, scented with oil of bergamot. **Lady Grey** is a softer, milder version with orange peel, lemon peel, and other citrus flavors added to yield a fresh light flavor.

    Oolong tea, from the Fujian Province in China, is created by a technique of partial rather than full oxidation. After withering, the tea is placed in muslin sacks and gently rolled, causing some oxidation to occur; this is repeated until the leaf turns darker green in appearance, resulting in a golden color with a toasty taste. **Darjeeling** tea comes from an area in the foothills of the Himalayan Mountains where high elevation gardens and sloped terrain produce distinctive teas that are harvested in three growing seasons called "flushes." Most Darjeeling teas come from the first and second flushes to yield a tea with a woody aroma and dry delicate taste.

    White tea, which is more delicate in flavor and more exclusive, is the least processed form of tea. It's picked from the first buds, which make it the rarest and most expensive of all teas. White Yunnan Silver Tips from China has a delicate floral taste and sweet aroma; it's offered at many of Ireland's luxury afternoon tea spots. **Green tea**—like Morgentau from China or Shizuoka Sencha from Japan—doesn't undergo the same withering and fermentation process used to make black tea; as a result, green tea is said to have more health benefits. **Pu-Erh tea,** a specially fermented tea from China's Yunnan province, is also regarded for its health benefits. It's the most oxidized form of tea, and because it mellows with age like fine wine, it's often very expensive.

Margaret M. Johnson

Monkey Business | Dreamstime.com

Chapter Two
Sandwiches and Savories

There are few hours in life more agreeable than the hour dedicated to the ceremony known as afternoon tea.

HENRY JAMES, AMERICAN NOVELIST

AFTERNOON tea, that lovely tradition where a fondness for tea and a penchant for sweets comes together most agreeably each afternoon, is one of life's little pleasures. The practice was established around 1840, a time when lunch was eaten early and dinner wasn't served until 8 or 9 o'clock in the evening. The story of its creation says that when Anna Maria, the 7th Duchess of Bedford, was feeling a bit hungry late one afternoon while on summer holiday at Woburn Abbey, she asked her maid to bring tea and a tray of bread-and-butter sandwiches to her room. Anna Maria enjoyed her "taking of tea" so much that she started inviting friends to join her for this new social event, one that gradually expanded to a menu that included assorted fruit breads and small pastries. In just a few decades, the custom was well established, and teashops and tearooms began opening for the enjoyment of the general public.

Tea sandwiches are the first course in a formal afternoon tea. This tea staple comes in all shapes and sizes, with fillings as simple as egg salad (known as egg mayonnaise in Ireland) topped with a few sprigs of watercress to more elaborate smoked salmon sandwiches layered with avocado purée arranged on homemade brown bread. Sandwiches are cut into delicate rounds, dainty triangles, or served open-faced as a *tartine*. To suggest that official "recipes" are required for such apparently simple assemblies seems unnecessary, but once you see these delicious sandwich ideas, you'll be delighted to serve them at your next gathering. In addition to sandwiches, you'll often find savory tarts and bite-size meat and cheese fritters sharing this course, especially in Northern Ireland tea rooms where homage is paid to the region's connection to British teatime traditions. To create a perfect tea sandwich, choose firm-textured bread, small rolls, croissants, or mini bagels. Once filled, cover sandwiches with a slightly dampened tea towel or paper towel and refrigerate.

SMOKED SALMON AND DILL TEA SANDWICHES

Makes 12

IRISH smoked salmon is one of the most popular ingredients for a tea sandwich. Spread bread slices with this tasty blend of cream cheese, butter, and horseradish and then top with fresh dill. Thinly sliced cucumbers or Red Onion Marmalade (pg. 31) are also delicious.

- 12 slices dark wheat or pumpernickel bread
- 3 oz. cream cheese, at room temperature
- 1 oz. butter, at room temperature
- 1 tbsp. prepared horseradish
- 1 tbsp. minced fresh dill, plus dill sprigs for filling
- 1 1/2 tbsp. fresh lemon juice
- 1/2 tsp. white pepper
- 4 oz. smoked salmon

1. With a serrated knife, trim and discard crusts from each bread slice; set aside.
2. In a food processor, combine cream cheese, butter, horseradish, 1 tablespoon dill, lemon juice, and pepper; process for 20 to 30 seconds, or until smooth.
3. Spread a thick layer of cream cheese mixture onto one side of 6 bread slices.
4. Cut salmon into 2-inch strips and arrange slices on top of cream cheese mixture. Place a few sprigs of dill over salmon and cover with remaining bread slices.
5. With a serrated knife, cut each sandwich into rectangles. Serve immediately or cover sandwiches with a damp tea towel or paper towel and refrigerate until ready to serve.

Bewley's

SMOKED SALMON TARTINE ON GUINNESS TREACLE BREAD

Makes 12

ERNEST Bewley opened his famous café on Grafton Street in 1927. The iconic building, described as a "Dublin landmark," once housed Whyte's Academy, a school whose pupils included Irish nationalist Robert Emmet, and the Duke of Wellington, who was twice the British Prime Minister. Irish poet Brendan Kennelly says, "Bewley's is the heart and the hearth of Dublin . . . walking into Bewley's never fails to give me the feeling that I am stepping into a home. The atmosphere is full of a lovely rattling music made up of cups and chatter, gossip and laughter, watchful eyes and gadabout tongues." This smoked salmon *tartine*, served on house-made Guinness and treacle bread, tops the menu at the newly refurbished café.

GUINNESS TREACLE BREAD
Makes 1 loaf

- 3/4 cups bread flour
- 3 cups whole wheat spelt flour
- 1/2 tsp. sea salt
- 1 1/2 tsp. baking soda
- 3/4 cup Guinness
- 2/3 cups buttermilk
- 1/4 cup sunflower oil
- 1 cup treacle or molasses

1. Preheat oven to 375°F. Butter a 9-inch loaf pan and dust with flour; tap out excess.
2. In large bowl, whisk together flours, salt, and baking soda.
3. In a medium bowl, whisk together Guinness, buttermilk, oil, and treacle or molasses. Make a well in center of flour mixture and stir in Guinness mixture until blended.
4. Transfer to prepared pan and bake for 50 minutes, or until a skewer inserted into center comes out clean.
5. Remove from oven and let cool on a wire rack for 30 minutes. Invert bread onto cutting board and then return to upright.

SANDWICHES
- 12 slices treacle bread
- 2 oz. butter or cream cheese, at room temperature
- 1 tbsp. horseradish
- 12 slices Irish smoked salmon
- Baby arugula or watercress, for garnish

1. Make sandwiches. With a serrated knife, cut bread into slices.
2. In a small bowl, combine butter or cream cheese with horseradish; spread on one side of each bread slice. Arrange salmon slices on top and garnish with arugula and watercress; serve immediately.

Kinsale
Free Range

These eggs are produced by hens
that have the freedom to roam &
forage on grass & cereals on our
family run farm.
Packed by: S O'Regan
Beechwood Farm, Ballyregan, Kinsale, Co. Cork.
www.beechwoodfarm.ie info@beechwoodfarm.ie
(086) 8292771. REG No: IE-04-223

Size

1IED13
1 = Free Range
IE = Produced in Rep. of Ireland
D = Co. Cork
13 - Flock Code

Tourism Ireland

EGG AND TOMATO TEA SANDWICHES

Makes 12

THIS egg salad sandwich is a classic in Irish homes and restaurants. Traditionalists will use white bread—Brennan's Premium White or Pat the Baker are two popular brands in Ireland—and cut each sandwich into four triangles, but whole wheat or rye bread also makes a delicious sandwich.

- 6 slices firm white bread
- 1 oz. butter, at room temperature
- 1 to 2 cherry tomatoes
- 2 hardboiled eggs
- 1 to 2 tbsp. chopped green onion
- 1 to 2 lettuce leaves, finely shredded
- 2 tbsp. mayonnaise
- Salt
- Ground black pepper
- Watercress

1. With a serrated knife, trim and discard crusts from each bread slice. Butter one side of each slice; set aside.
2. Cut tomatoes in half and scoop out flesh and seeds; dice tomatoes.
3. In a medium bowl, mash eggs. Stir in tomatoes, onion, lettuce, mayonnaise, salt, and pepper until smooth.
4. Spread a thick layer of egg mixture onto buttered side of each slice of bread. Top with watercress and cover with the remaining slices.
5. With a serrated knife, cut each sandwich diagonally into 4 triangles. Serve immediately or cover with a damp tea towel or paper towels and refrigerate until ready to serve.

Funandrejs | Dreamstime.com

CUCUMBER AND HERBED GOAT CHEESE TEA SANDWICHES

Makes 12

Cucumber sandwiches are nearly obligatory in the first course of afternoon tea. Whipped cream cheese is a perfect companion to thinly sliced cucumbers, but herbed cheese and butter elevate the sandwiches to special occasion status. English cucumbers, which have thinner skin and smaller seeds than the common slicing cucumber, are generally preferred because of their sweeter flavor.

- 1 English cucumber, thinly sliced
- Salt, for sprinkling
- White vinegar, for sprinkling
- 12 slices firm white bread
- 8 oz. cream cheese, at room temperature
- 4 oz. Irish goat cheese, at room temperature
- 1/2 tsp. lemon pepper
- Sea salt
- 1/3 cup milk
- 1/2 tsp. minced fresh thyme leaves
- 1/2 tsp. minced fresh tarragon
- 3 tbsp. minced fresh flatleaf parsley
- 1 cup watercress leaves

1. Put cucumber slices into a colander and sprinkle with salt and vinegar; toss gently to coat slices. Leave for 30 minutes to drain excess moisture.
2. With a serrated knife, trim and discard crusts from each bread slice; set aside.
3. In a medium bowl, combine cream cheese, goat cheese, lemon pepper, salt, and milk. With an electric mixer, beat until blended. Stir in thyme, tarragon, and parsley until smooth.
4. Spread a thick layer of cream cheese mixture onto one side of 6 bread slices. Top with watercress and overlap cucumber slices on top; cover with the remaining bread slice.
5. With a serrated knife, cut each sandwich diagonally into 2 triangles. Serve immediately or cover with a damp tea towel or paper towels and refrigerate until ready to serve.

Margaret M. Johnson

ROAST BEEF TEA SANDWICHES WITH RED ONION MARMALADE

Makes 12

IRISH beef is among the best in the world. Thinly sliced and topped with the sweet-salty-savory condiment known as Red Onion Marmalade or Red Onion Jam, these sandwiches make a bold statement. The marmalade is also delicious on smoked salmon sandwiches and with ham and cheese.

RED ONION MARMALADE

Makes 1 cup

- 1 oz. butter
- 2 tbsp. olive oil
- 2 large red onions, thinly sliced
- 1/4 cup (packed) light brown sugar
- 1/2 tsp. fresh thyme
- Sea salt
- Ground black pepper
- 3/4 cups dry red wine
- 3/4 cup malt vinegar

1. In a large saucepan over medium heat, melt butter and oil; add onions and stir until coated. Stir in sugar, thyme, salt, and pepper. Reduce heat to medium-low and cook, stirring occasionally, for 25 to 30 minutes, or until onions are soft and caramelized.
2. Stir in wine and vinegar. Continue to cook, stirring occasionally, for 30 to 35 minutes, or until mixture is thick and syrupy.
3. Remove from heat and let mixture cool in pan. Serve on sandwiches, or transfer to plastic containers, cover, and refrigerate for up to 2 weeks.

SANDWICHES

- 12 mini croissants, cut in half horizontally
- 1 cup baby arugula
- 1/2 pound thinly sliced roast beef

1. With a serrated knife, cut croissants in half. Spread a thick layer of marmalade onto bottom half of croissants; top with arugula. Arrange roast beef slices on top and cover with top half of croissants. Serve immediately or cover with a damp tea towel or paper towels and refrigerate until ready to serve.

Margaret M. Johnson

HAM AND CHEDDAR TEA SANDWICHES WITH TOMATO CHUTNEY

Makes 12

ANOTHER well-loved sandwich combination is ham and cheddar cheese—simply delicious spread with mayonnaise, whole grain or Dijon mustard. The sandwiches join the afternoon tea course when you make them on dark wheat bread or Mrs. Tea's Seed Bread (pg. 35) and spread them with this piquant tomato chutney. At some tea spots in Northern Ireland, you might find these sandwiches topped with the beloved British chutney known as Branston Pickle.

TOMATO CHUTNEY

Makes 2 cups

- 1 cup sugar
- 1 1/2 cups cider vinegar
- 2 tsp. kosher salt
- 1 tsp. ground cardamom
- 1 tsp. ground ginger
- 1/4 tsp. ground cloves
- 1/2 tsp. mustard seeds
- 1 1/2 pounds (6 to 7 medium) plum tomatoes, quartered
- 1 medium onion, chopped
- 2 tbsp. minced garlic
- 1 tbsp. olive oil
- 1/2 cup golden raisins
- Ground black pepper

1. In a large saucepan over medium-low heat, combine sugar, vinegar, salt, cardamom, ginger, cloves, mustard seed, and tomatoes. Bring the mixture slowly to boil, stirring until sugar is dissolved.
2. Add onion, garlic, oil, raisins, and pepper. Reduce heat to simmer and cook, uncovered, for 1 to 1 1/4 hours, or until the mixture thickens. Stir frequently, and when tomato skins separate from pulp, remove with a fork and discard. Remove from heat and let mixture cool in pan. Serve on sandwiches, or transfer to plastic containers, cover, and refrigerate for up to 2 weeks.

SANDWICHES

- 8 slices dark wheat or multi-grain bread
- 1/4 pound sliced Cheddar cheese
- 1/4 pound sliced ham

1. Spread a thick layer of chutney onto one side of 3 bread slices; top with 2 slices of cheese. Arrange 2 slices of ham on top and cover with remaining bread slices. With a serrated knife, cut sandwiches into 3 rectangles. Serve immediately or cover with a damp tea towel or paper towels and refrigerate until ready to serve.

HONEY ROAST HAM AND APPLE TEA SANDWICHES WITH TEA-INFUSED APPLE CHUTNEY

Makes 12

At Cupán Tae, a unique tea shop/café with locations in Galway (8 Quay Lane) and Westport (Bridge Street), County Mayo, you can have your tea in a cup, of course, but you can also have your tea in a scone, a piece of carrot cake, or in this flavorful apple chutney because everything on the menu is infused with tea! Owner Allison McArdle is passionate about tea—she sells more than 50 loose varieties in the shop—and takes that love a step further by using tea to enhance the flavors of her food in the same way a chef uses spices. In this apple chutney, she uses Emerald Isle tea, a full-bodied blend with tastes of whiskey, cocoa, and a touch of vanilla—a mix that evokes memories of the West of Ireland—but you can substitute your personal favorite tea. The chutney is also delicious on a ham and cheese sandwich or on a cheese board.

APPLE CHUTNEY
Makes 2 cups

- 5 tsp. Emerald Isle tea
- 1 1/3 cups apple cider vinegar
- 1 1/2 pounds apples, chopped finely
- 1 1/2 cups (packed) light brown sugar
- 1 3/4 cups raisins
- 1 tsp. mustard seeds
- 1 onion, chopped
- 1 tsp. ground ginger
- 1/2 tsp. ground cinnamon
- 1/2 tsp. salt

1. In a large saucepan over medium heat, combine tea and vinegar. Heat for about 3 minutes, and then remove from heat and let cool completely.
2. Return saucepan to medium heat. Add apples, brown sugar, raisins, mustard seed, onion, ginger, cinnamon, and salt. Cook for 1 to 1 1/4 hours, or until the mixture thickens. Remove from heat and let mixture cool in pan. Serve on sandwiches, or transfer to plastic containers, cover, and refrigerate for up to 2 weeks.

SANDWICHES
- 8 slices wheat or multi-grain bread
- 1/4 pound sliced honey roast ham
- 1 apple, cored and thinly sliced

1. Spread a thick layer of chutney onto one side of 4 bread slices; top with 2 slices of ham. Arrange 3 slices of apple on top and cover with remaining bread slices. With a serrated knife, cut sandwiches into 3 rectangles. Serve immediately or cover with a damp tea towel or paper towels and refrigerate until ready to serve.

MRS. TEA'S SEED BREAD

Makes 1 loaf

ASHFORD Castle in County Mayo needs no introduction when it comes to elegant afternoon tea service. Smoked salmon sandwiches arrive on this nutty, aromatic, crusty brown bread, a recipe from Mrs. Beatrice Tollman, founder of the Red Carnation Hotel Collection—a five-star luxury group that includes Ashford. You can pick up a loaf at Mrs. Tea's Boutique and Bakery on the Ashford estate or buy the ingredients for it that are cleverly packaged in a bottle ready to take home and bake yourself. The bread is also delicious toasted and spread with butter and jam for breakfast.

- 1 1/3 cups whole wheat flour
- 1/4 cup all-purpose flour
- 1/4 cup muesli
- 1/2 tsp. baking soda
- 1/4 tsp. salt
- 1/3 cup raisins
- 1/2 cup flax seeds
- 1/2 cup pumpkin seeds
- 1/2 cup chopped walnuts
- 2 1/4 cups plain yogurt
- 1/3 cup sunflower oil
- 1/4 cup honey

1. Preheat oven to 375°F. Butter a 9-inch loaf pan and dust with flour; tap out excess.
2. In large bowl, combine flours, muesli, baking soda, salt, raisins, flax seeds, pumpkin seeds, and walnuts; stir to blend.
3. In a medium bowl, whisk together yogurt, oil, and honey. Stir yogurt mixture into flour mixture; mix well.
4. Transfer to prepared pan. Bake for 1 hour, or until skewer inserted into center comes out clean.
5. Remove from oven and let cool on a wire rack for 30 minutes. Invert bread onto cutting board and then return to upright. With a serrated knife, cut bread into slices.

Ratmaner | Dreamstime. com

Ezumeimages | Dreamstime.com

CHICKEN, BACON, AND TOMATO TEA SANDWICHES

Makes 12

MANY afternoon tea rooms subscribe to the theory that there's no need for a sandwich recipe *per se*, as quality ingredients and good bread make a good sandwich: think slices of roast chicken, strips of crisp bacon, and sliced ripe tomatoes. For a great sandwich, top this with avocado mayonnaise.

- 1 avocado, peeled and pitted
- 4 tbsp. mayonnaise
- 1 tbsp. fresh lemon juice
- Salt
- Ground black pepper
- 12 slices wheat bread
- 4 slices roasted chicken
- 4 slices bacon
- 4 slices tomato
- Baby greens

1. In a small bowl, mash avocado; whisk in mayonnaise, lemon juice, salt, and pepper. Refrigerate for up to 1 day.
2. With a serrated knife, trim bread slices and discard crusts. Spread a thick layer of avocado mayonnaise onto one side of 6 bread slices. Arrange slices of chicken, bacon, and tomato on top; cover with baby greens. Cover with remaining bread slices.
3. With a serrated knife, cut sandwiches in half. Serve immediately or cover with a damp tea towel or paper towels and refrigerate until ready to serve.

LCC54613 | Dreamstime.com

CORONATION CHICKEN SALAD TEA SANDWICHES

Makes 12

MANGO chutney—a cooked blend of fruit, vinegar, sugar, herbs, and spices—is combined with chicken salad and curry powder for these tasty tea sandwiches. The recipe, developed for Queen Elizabeth's 1953 coronation luncheon, is popular in tea rooms throughout Ireland.

- 2 cups chopped roasted chicken
- 5 tbsp. mayonnaise
- 1 tsp. mild curry powder
- 1 1/2 tbsp. mango chutney
- 1/3 cup golden raisins
- 1/3 cup slivered almonds
- Salt
- Ground black pepper
- 12 mini croissants
- Baby arugula

1. In a medium bowl, combine chicken, mayonnaise, curry powder, chutney, raisins, almonds, salt, and pepper; stir to blend.
2. With a serrated knife, cut croissants in half. Spread a thick layer of salad mixture onto bottom half of croissants; top with arugula. Cover with top half of croissants. Serve immediately or cover with a damp tea towel or paper towel and refrigerate until ready to serve.

Olena Danileiko | Dreamstime.com

GOAT CHEESE AND TOMATO TARTLETS

Makes 30

PRE-BAKED phyllo shells are the answer to a cook's prayer when it comes to making savory teatime tartlets. With a quick sauté of onions in garlic and herb butter, these cheese and tomato tarts are ready for your tea in less than 20 minutes.

- 2 tbsp. garlic and herb butter, such as Kerrygold brand
- 1 tbsp. olive oil
- 1 tbsp. finely chopped onion
- 1 tbsp. dry white wine
- Salt
- Ground black pepper
- 30 mini phyllo shells, such as Athens brand
- 2 oz. goat cheese, crumbled
- 6 to 8 cherry tomatoes, thinly sliced
- 1 tbsp. grated parmesan cheese
- Finely chopped basil, for garnish

1. Preheat oven to 325°F. In a small skillet over medium-low heat, heat butter and oil. Add onion and cook for 2 to 3 minutes, or until soft but not browned. Stir in wine, salt, and pepper; cook for 1 minute longer.
2. Arrange shells on a baking sheet. Spoon onion mixture into each shell and cover with goat cheese. Top each with a tomato slice and sprinkle with Parmesan cheese. Bake for 10 to 12 minutes, or until filling is warm and tomatoes are lightly browned.
3. Remove from oven and garnish with basil. Serve warm or at room temperature.

TRUFFLED WILD MUSHROOM TARTLETS

Makes 30

THESE quiche-like mushroom tarts, a delicious mix of white and specialty mushrooms—chanterelles, porcini, morels, Portobello, crimini, shiitakes, oysters, enoki—bring previously exotic mushroom varieties to the savory side of the sandwich course.

- 1 tbsp. canola oil
- 8 oz. mixed wild mushrooms, roughly chopped
- 1 clove shallot, minced
- 1 tbsp. white truffle oil
- 1 tbsp. minced fresh flat-leaf parsley
- 30 mini phyllo shells, such as Athens brand
- 1 large egg
- 1/2 cup half and half
- Grated parmesan, for sprinkling
- Fresh parsley, for garnish

1. Preheat oven to 350°F. In a large skillet over medium heat, heat oil. Add mushrooms and shallots and cook for 3 to 4 minutes, or until mushrooms are soft but not browned; stir in truffle oil and parsley.
2. Arrange shells on a baking sheet. Spoon mushroom mixture into each shell. In a small bowl, whisk together egg and half and half. Spoon 1 teaspoon of egg mixture over mushrooms; sprinkle with cheese. Bake for 12 to 15 minutes, or until filling is set.
3. Remove from oven and garnish with a sprig of parsley. Serve warm or at room temperature.

CASHEL BLUE CHEESECAKES

Makes 12

CASHEL Blue cheese, produced in County Tipperary, is Ireland's first and most popular blue cheese. You'll find it on cheese boards, in soups, on sandwiches, and in this savory cheesecake with a nutty crust that's a perfect addition to the savories course.

- 1 1/2 cups digestive biscuits, such as McVities's or Carr's brand
- 1/4 cup walnuts
- 1 oz. unsalted butter, melted
- 4 oz. Cashel Blue cheese, crumbled
- 8 oz. cream cheese, at room temperature
- 2 large eggs
- 1 tsp. minced fresh chives
- Salt
- Ground black pepper
- Finely chopped walnuts, for garnish

1. Preheat oven to 325°F. Coat the cups of a standard cupcake pan with nonstick spray.
2. In a food processor, combine biscuits, walnuts, and butter; pulse 4 to 5 times, or until mixture resembles fine crumbs. Press mixture into bottom of each cup; bake for 5 to 6 minutes, or until lightly browned. Let cool.
3. In a medium bowl, beat blue cheese and cream cheese with an electric mixer until smooth. Add eggs, one at a time, beating well after each addition. Stir in chives, salt, and pepper. Spoon into cups and bake for about 20 minutes, or until filling is set and tops are golden. Remove from oven; let cool 1 hour.
4. To loosen, run a sharp knife around the sides of each cheesecake and remove; sprinkle with walnuts.

Bushmills Inn

PORK AND APPLE SAUSAGE ROLLS

Makes 36

THE Bushmills Inn is an historic coaching inn located in the heart of Northern Ireland's Causeway Coast in Country Antrim. The "quietly luxurious" hotel is only a short distance from local attractions that include the famous Giant's Causeway, reputed to be giant Finn McCool's steppingstones to Scotland; seventeenth century Dunluce Castle, headquarters of the McDonnell Clan; and the Old Bushmills Distillery, the oldest working distillery in Ireland. Afternoon tea is served at The Loft, part of the original coach house with whitewashed walls. As part of the savories course, these pork and apple sausage rolls are served with a demitasse of soup.

- 2 sheets frozen puff pastry, such as Pepperidge Farm brand
- 2 pounds bulk pork sausage meat
- 2 Bramley apples, grated
- 1 Granny Smith apple, grated
- Salt
- Ground black pepper
- 1 large egg mixed with 1 tbsp. water, for egg wash

1. Preheat oven to 425°F. Line 2 baking sheets with parchment paper.
2. Thaw pastry at room temperature for 40 minutes. Unfold on a lightly floured surface and cut along fold lines to create 6 strips.
3. In a large bowl, combine sausage meat with apples; season with salt and pepper. Place a 1 1/2-inch-thick roll of mixture down the center of each pastry sheet. Brush sides of each sheet with egg wash and roll to seal.
4. Cut each roll into 6 pieces and place seam-side down on prepared pans. Brush tops with additional egg wash, and with the tip of a sharp knife, prick 2 to 3 slits in each to allow steam to escape. Bake for 15 to 18 minutes, or until the rolls are puffed and golden. Serve immediately or at room temperature.

HAM HOCK FRITTERS WITH PLUM AND CHILI JAM

Makes 8 to 12

ANOTHER delicious addition to the savory course are these ham hock fritters served at Lough Erne Resort in County Fermanagh. Head chef Noel McMeel is known for his eclectic menus, so it comes as no surprise to find these tasty, bite-size fritters served at the resort's "Taste of Lough Erne" afternoon tea. Try them with plum and chili jam or your favorite fruit chutney.

PLUM AND CHILI JAM

Makes 2 cups

- 1 tbsp. olive oil
- 1 large red onion, chopped
- 6 red chilis, seeds removed, finely chopped
- 2 garlic cloves
- 1 pound plums, stones removed, quartered
- 1/2 cup balsamic vinegar
- 1 cup (packed) light brown sugar

1. In a medium saucepan over medium-low heat, heat olive oil. Add onion and cook for about 5 minutes, or until soft but not browned. Stir in chilis and garlic and cook for 5 minutes.
2. Add plums and vinegar and cook for about 10 minutes, removing the skins as they separate from the plums. Stir in sugar and cook, stirring frequently, for 30 to 40 minutes, or until the temperature reaches 220°F on a candy thermometer. Serve with fritters, or transfer to plastic containers, cover, and refrigerate for up to 2 weeks.

FRITTERS

- 1 ham hock
- 1 large russet potato
- 5 oz. Cheddar cheese
- 3 tbsp. chopped fresh chives
- 1/2 tsp. Dijon mustard
- Flour, for dredging
- 1 egg mixed with 1 tbsp. water, for dredging
- Breadcrumbs, for dredging
- Canola oil, for frying

1. In a large saucepan over medium heat, cover ham hock with water; bring to a boil. Reduce heat to low and cook for about 2 hours, or until tender and falling off bone. With a slotted spoon, remove from heat and let cool.
2. Preheat oven to 350°F. Bake potato for about 1 hour, or until tender when pierced with the tip of a sharp knife. Cut in half and scoop out potato; transfer to medium bowl and mash. Stir in chives, cheese, and mustard.
3. Pull ham from bone, and with 2 forks, shred ham; cut into small pieces and then stir into potato mixture. Shape mixture into 2-inch cylinders. Roll each cylinder in flour, then in beaten eggs, and then in breadcrumbs; transfer to a baking sheet. Repeat with remaining mixture.

4. In a medium skillet, heat oil to 375°F. Working in batches, fry fritters for about 2 minutes, or until golden. Transfer to a paper towel-lined tray to drain. Heat oil to 375°F for each new batch. Serve fritters with jam.

AFTERNOON TEA OR HIGH TEA: THERE IS A DIFFERENCE

THE terms "afternoon tea" and "high tea" are often confused, although in the past they were actually a peek into your social standing. Afternoon tea originated as a small elegant meal served between a light lunch and late dinner—usually between 3 and 5 p.m.—and was mainly a practice of the aristocracy, who enjoyed a leisurely lifestyle.

Afternoon tea cuisine eventually expanded in range to include wafer thin, crust-less sandwiches, shrimp or fish pâtés, toasted breads with jams, and regional pastries such as scones and tea bread. Regardless of the menu, the emphasis was always on presentation and conversation.

High tea, on the other hand, has always been a more substantial meal—often including sausages or meat pies—and was really an early dinner or supper more suited to the middle and lower classes after a long day at work. High tea, sometimes called meat tea, was the main meal of the day for the working classes and consisted of full dinner items such as roast beef and mashed potatoes and, of course, tea. Many Irish households today still refer to the evening meal as "tea" despite what's on the menu.

Cupán Tae

At Cupán Tae, a unique tea shop/café with locations in Galway and Westport, you can have your tea in a cup, of course, but you can also have your tea in your chicken salad, or your scone, or your pastry because everything on the menu is infused with tea! Owner Allison McArdle is passionate about it—she sells a number of loose varieties in the shop—and takes that love a step further by using tea to enhance the flavors of her food in the same way a chef uses spices.

Quanthem | Dreamstime.com

Avoca Café

CHAPTER THREE

SCONES, TEA BREADS, AND TRAY BAKES

People drink coffee on the go; you take a moment for tea.

PAUL O'TOOLE, MASTER BLENDER, BEWLEY'S TEA

THE second course in a formal afternoon tea is a selection of scones served with butter, fruit preserves, clotted cream and, sometimes, lemon curd. Some tea spots might also offer savory scones made with cheese, sundried tomatoes, or fresh herbs. Traditional tea breads and "bracks"—speckled fruit breads—will be offered at some formal tea events, but these breads are a mainstay for casual teas at home.

According to the late Irish cookery writer Theodora FitzGibbon, these breads, which are not overly sweet, are a reminder of one's Celtic heritage: "All the Celtic countries—Ireland, Scotland, Wales, even Brittany—have many things in common, including a surprising number of foods general to all. There is little to choose between the Barmrack of Ireland, the Bara Brith of Wales, and the Selkirk Bannock of Scotland," any one of which might appear at teatime in Ireland. Despite what they're called, many of these breads begin with a lengthy soak of dried fruits in tea, and in some recipes a bit of brandy, rum, or sherry is also added.

In addition to a tea bread or brack, selections from tray bakes—sweets that are baked in a sheet pan and then cut into individual squares or slices for serving—are also essential at teatime. Home cooks rely on them for informal teatime gatherings, and they love to mix-and-match seasonal fruits with different crumble toppings or to transform traditional sweets like Bakewell tart into larger portion Bakewell slices. Irish bakeries big and small are always reliable sources for teatime scones and tea breads, although every self-respecting hostess generally prefers to showcase her own recipes: "Breads and cakes are the Irishwoman's true forte," FitzGibbon later claimed, "she loves both making them and eating them . . . they are probably the most traditional food which still exist in Ireland."

AVOCA SCONES

Makes 12 to 18

AVOCA, a name synonymous with colorful handwoven Irish woolens, is one of the world's oldest surviving manufacturing companies and Ireland's oldest weaving mill. In the 1970s, the Pratt family purchased the centuries-old property in rural County Wicklow and restored it to what is now one of Ireland's most exciting retail names. Their cafes, restaurants, and food markets are an integral part of Avoca shops across Ireland, and these scones are among the most popular to serve with *cupán tea*.

- 4 cups self-rising flour
- 1/4 tsp. baking powder
- 1/4 tsp. salt
- 1/4 cup sugar
- 4 oz. cold unsalted butter, cut into pieces
- 1 large egg, beaten
- 1/4 cup heavy (whipping) cream
- 1 cup milk, plus more if needed
- 1 egg beaten with 1 tbsp. water, for brushing tops
- Softened butter and jam, for serving
- Clotted cream and lemon curd, for serving (optional)

1. Preheat oven to 350°F. Line a baking sheet with parchment paper.
2. In a large bowl, sift together flour, baking powder, and salt; stir in sugar. With a pastry blender or your fingers, cut or work in butter until mixture resembles coarse crumbs. Make a well in center, and with a wooden spoon, stir in egg, cream, and milk until mixture forms soft dough.
3. Transfer dough to a lightly floured surface, and with floured hands, knead gently to bring dough together. Roll out or pat dough into a 3/4-inch-thick-round. With a 2 1/2-inch biscuit cutter, cut out rounds. Reroll scraps and cut out additional rounds. Transfer scones to prepared pan and brush tops with egg wash.
4. Bake for 15 to 18 minutes, or until scones are risen and tops are golden brown. Remove from oven and let cool on a wire rack for 10 minutes. Serve with butter and jam.

Shelbourne Hotel

TEA AT THE SHELBOURNE

THE Shelbourne Hotel on St. Stephen's Green has been the social center of Dublin since it opened its doors in 1824. This historic building has always been an integral part of the city's literary, social, culinary, and artistic traditions, including serving as the venue for the drafting of the Irish Constitution in 1922. The Lord Mayor's Lounge, where afternoon tea is served daily, is a place where the ritual is so fiercely followed that not even the Easter Rising of 1916 could keep the fine ladies of Dublin from their tea and cakes. This historical note was recently added to the afternoon tea menu:

"In her book *The Shelbourne*, Irish author Elizabeth Bowen described how the unruffled gentlewomen arrived at the hotel that fateful Easter Monday, dressed in their best and sporting their new Easter bonnets:

> . . . bobbling millinery and smiling faces
> appeared on the farther side of the barricades;
> and scrambling nimbly round the obstruction,
> the tea-time parties began to come surging in.

While there was some question of whether tea might be more safely served in the library than in the 'sunny and splendid' drawing room, there was never any question of cancelling the event. Tea must and would be served and whatever was happening outside the walls of The Shelbourne could wait. The pots of tea and pastries were brought out, spirits were high, and civilized conversation flowed. When a stray bullet flew through the window and clipped one petal of a rose in a lady's hat, the guests finally agreed to move to another room . . . but they took their tea with them" . . . and probably these scones, a staple on the menu for decades.

THE LORD MAYOR'S BUTTERMILK SCONES

Makes 16 to 18

- 3 1/2 cups flour
- 1 tsp. baking soda
- 1 tsp. salt
- 1 tsp. sugar
- 1 oz. cold butter, cut into pieces
- 2/3 cup buttermilk
- 1 large egg, beaten
- Softened butter and jam, for serving
- Clotted cream and lemon curd, for serving

1. Preheat oven to 325°F. Line a baking sheet with parchment paper.
2. In a large bowl, sift together flour, baking soda, and salt; stir in sugar. With a pastry blender or your fingers, cut or work in butter until mixture resembles coarse crumbs. Make a well in center, and with a wooden spoon, stir in buttermilk and egg until mixture forms soft dough.
3. Transfer dough to a lightly floured surface. Roll out or pat dough into a 1-inch-thick round. With a 2 1/2-inch biscuit cutter, cut into rounds; reroll scraps and cut out additional rounds.
4. Transfer scones to prepared pan and bake for 15 minutes, or until scones are risen and tops are golden brown. Remove from oven and let cool on a wire rack for 10 minutes. Serve spread with butter, jam, clotted cream, and lemon curd.

CRANBERRY-GINGER DROP SCONES

Makes 10 to 12

THIS recipe breaks from the traditional round scone shape and requires no kneading, rolling, or cutting. Simply mix up the dough and drop onto a baking sheet. Another break from tradition, the recipe uses yogurt instead of either buttermilk, milk, or cream; crystallized ginger chips add a bit of zing!

- 2 cups flour
- 1/2 tsp. salt
- 1/4 cup sugar
- 1 tbsp. baking powder
- 3 oz. cold butter, cut into pieces
- 3/4 cup sweetened dried cranberries, chopped
- 1/4 cup crystallized ginger, chopped
- 1 tbsp. lemon zest
- 2 large eggs, beaten
- 1/2 cup vanilla yogurt
- 1 tsp. vanilla bean paste
- Milk, for brushing tops
- Softened butter, for serving
- Clotted cream and lemon curd, for serving (optional)

1. Preheat oven to 375°F. Line a baking sheet with parchment paper.
2. In a large bowl, whisk together flour, salt, sugar, and baking powder. With a pastry blender or your fingers, cut or work in butter until mixture resembles coarse crumbs; stir in cranberries, ginger, and lemon zest.
3. In a medium bowl, whisk together eggs, yogurt, and vanilla. Make a well in center, and with a wooden spoon, stir into dry ingredients until mixture forms soft dough. With a cookie dough scoop or large spoon, drop dough onto prepared pan, leaving about 2 inches between each; brush tops with milk. Bake for 20 to 24 minutes, or until scones are risen and tops are golden brown. Remove from oven and let cool on a wire rack for 10 minutes. Serve spread with butter.

Creantive | Dreams-time.com

BUNRATTY FOLK PARK SCONES

Makes 18

BUNRATTY Folk Park, situated behind the medieval castle in the village of Bunratty, County Clare, is a charming recreation of life in nineteenth century Ireland. The park, which features a village street, farmhouses, blacksmith forge, and a display of period agricultural machinery, not only preserves Ireland's architectural history but also the hearty and wholesome recipes of its culinary past. During the spring and summer months, visitors can meet *Bean An Tí* (woman of the house) in the pretty pink farmhouse kitchen where she demonstrates how to make these delicious scones. This recipe is for classic raisin scones, but for a variation you can substitute other dried fruits like currants, cranberries, or apricots.

- 4 cups flour
- 2 tsp. baking powder
- 1 tsp. baking soda
- 1 tbsp. sugar
- 1/4 tsp. salt
- 2 oz. cold butter, cut into pieces
- 1/2 cup raisins
- 2 large eggs, beaten
- 2 cups buttermilk
- 1/4 cup heavy (whipping) cream, for brushing tops
- Softened butter and jam, for serving
- Clotted cream and lemon curd, for serving (optional)

1. Preheat oven to 400° F. Line a baking sheet with parchment paper.
2. In a large bowl, whisk together flour, baking powder, baking soda, sugar, and salt. With a pastry blender or your fingers, cut or work in butter until mixture resembles coarse crumbs; stir in raisins. Make a well in center, and with a wooden spoon, stir in egg and buttermilk until mixture forms soft dough.
3. Transfer dough to a lightly floured surface, and with floured hands knead in raisins. Roll out or pat dough into a 1/2-inch-thick round. With a 2 1/2-inch biscuit cutter, cut into rounds. Reroll scraps and cut out additional rounds.
4. Transfer scones to prepared pan and brush tops with cream. Bake for 18 to 20 minutes, or until scones are risen and tops are golden brown. Remove from oven and let cool on a wire rack for 10 minutes. Serve spread with butter and jam.

BLUEBERRY SCONES

Makes 16

When blueberries are in season, they often replace raisins or currants in fruit scones. This recipe also diverts from the traditional shape as the scones are baked in a scone pan that produces perfectly shaped little wedges.

- 1 1/2 cups all-purpose flour
- 1 1/2 cups cake flour
- 1/2 cup sugar
- 1 1/2 tbsp. baking powder
- 3/4 tsp. salt
- 2 tbsp. lemon zest
- 4 oz. cold butter, cut into small pieces
- 2 large eggs
- 3/4 cups heavy (whipping) cream
- 1/4 cup buttermilk
- 1 cup fresh blueberries
- 1 large egg mixed with 1 tbsp. milk, for brushing tops
- Softened butter, for serving
- Clotted cream and lemon curd, for serving (optional)

1. Preheat oven to 350° F. Coat a mini cast iron scone pan with nonstick cooking spray.
2. In a large bowl, whisk together flours, sugar, baking powder, salt, and lemon zest. With a pastry blender or your fingers, cut or work in butter until mixture resembles coarse crumbs.
3. In a medium bowl, whisk together eggs, cream, and buttermilk. Make a well in center, and with a wooden spoon, stir into flour mixture until mixture forms soft dough; fold in blueberries.
4. Spoon batter into prepared pan and brush tops with egg wash. Bake for 30 to 32 minutes, or until scones are risen and tops are golden brown. Remove from oven and let cool on a wire rack for 10 minutes. Serve spread with butter.

Nicole Franz | Dreamstime.com

BALLYMAQUIRKE FRUIT FARM KANTURK CO. CORK

HOMEMADE
RASPBERRY JAM
Net Weight: 350g

BALLYMAQUIRKE FRUIT FARM KANTURK CO. CORK

HOMEMADE
SEVILLE ORANGE MARMALADE
Net Weight: 350g

BALLYMAQUIRKE FRUIT FARM KANTURK CO. CORK

HOMEMADE
RASPBERRY JAM
Net Weight: 350g

BALLYMAQUIRKE FRUIT FARM KANTURK CO. CORK

HOMEMADE
BLACKCURRANT JAM
Net Weight: 350g

Margaret M. Johnson

TEATIME ESSENTIALS

I T's impossible to think of eating a scone without butter or jam—strawberry, raspberry, blackcurrant, or orange marmalade among the most popular—and *nearly* impossible to think of eating one without clotted cream and lemon curd, too. If you'd like to make your own rather than buy any of these teatime essentials, you'll love these recipes.

STRAWBERRY JAM
Makes 4 (1/2-pint) jars

- 2 1/4 pounds strawberries, rinsed and hulled
- 2 1/4 cups sugar
- 1/2 cup fresh lemon juice

1. Sterilize four 1/2-pint canning jars and lids (see Note).
2. In a large nonreactive saucepan, combine strawberries and sugar; sprinkle lemon juice on top. Leave for 10 to 15 minutes.
3. Turn heat to medium-low and cook, stirring gently, for 5 to 6 minutes, or until sugar dissolves. Increase heat to high and bring to a rapid boil. Reduce heat to medium-high and continue to boil, stirring frequently, for 20 to 25 minutes, or until mixture thickens and temperature registers 220°F on a candy thermometer; skim off any foam that develops.
4. Ladle mixture into prepared jars, filling to within 1/4-inch of top. Wipe rims with a dampened cloth and seal with lids.

Note: To sterilize jars and lids, run them through a high heat or sanitize cycle of your dishwasher, or put them in a large pot of water, bring to a boil, and let water boil for about 5 minutes. Turn heat down to simmer and leave jars and lids in water until ready to fill. Dry thoroughly just before filling.

LEMON CURD
Makes about 1 3/4 cups

Lemon curd is a rich, tart, thick spread that has been associated with afternoon tea since the eighteenth century. It's delicious spread on scones, toast, English muffins, or crumpets, but you can also blend it with whipped cream or cream cheese to use as a filling for tarts, pies, and cakes.

- 3 large eggs
- 1 cup sugar
- 4 oz. cold butter, cut into pieces
- 1 tbsp. grated lemon zest
- 1/2 cup fresh lemon juice

1. In the top of a double boiler set over simmering water, whisk eggs until frothy. Stir in sugar until blended; add butter, lemon zest, and juice.
2. Cook over medium heat, stirring constantly, for 15 to 20 minutes, or until mixture thickens and coats back of a spoon. Pour into 2 small jars; cool to room temperature. Cover and refrigerate for up to 1 week.

CLOTTED CREAM

Makes 1 cup

Traditionally made by gently simmering large vats of milk until a thick layer of cream can be skimmed off the top, authentic clotted cream has the consistency of soft butter. Also known as Devon, Cornish, or English clotted cream, it's sold in small jars in most supermarkets; however, you can substitute crème fraîche, mascarpone cheese, or make your own from one of these recipes.

- 2/3 cups heavy (whipping) cream
- 1 oz. cold unsalted butter

1. In a medium saucepan over medium-low heat, combine cream and butter. With a wooden spoon, stir gently until mixture simmers (do not let it boil). Cook, stirring constantly, for 20 to 25 minutes, or until mixture is reduced by half and starts to thicken.
2. Remove from heat, transfer to a shallow glass dish, and let cool completely. Cover and refrigerate for at least 24 hours. Just before serving, whip cream until mixture is smooth and thick. Store unused clotted cream in refrigerator for up to 1 week.

MOCK CLOTTED CREAM

Makes about 1 1/2 cups

This clotted cream recipe requires only a simple beating of heavy cream, a pinch of sugar, and mascarpone, a buttery rich double cream cheese made from cow's milk.

- 1 cup heavy (whipping) cream
- 1/2 cup mascarpone cheese
- Pinch of sugar

1. In a medium bowl, beat cream, mascarpone, and sugar until thick. Transfer to a glass jar, cover, and refrigerate for 2 to 3 hours, or until chilled. Store unused clotted cream in refrigerator for up to 1 week.

MARMALADE TEA LOAF

Makes 2 loaves

Even though marmalade was "invented" by Scotsman James Keiller, the Irish have a great fondness for this delicious orange jam, whether it's used to spread on breads and scones or baked in tea breads and cakes. For a little kick, you might be tempted to use one of Ireland's delicious whiskey-flavored marmalades in this teatime bread.

- 1 cup sugar
- 1 cup milk
- 1/2 cup golden raisins
- 1/2 cup orange marmalade
- 4 oz. unsalted butter
- 2 cups self-rising flour
- 1/2 tsp. baking soda
- 1 tsp. pumpkin pie spice or Mixed Spice (see Note)
- 1/4 tsp. salt
- 1 large egg, beaten
- Softened butter, for serving

1. In a medium saucepan over medium heat, bring sugar, milk, raisins, marmalade, and butter to boil; stir well. Remove from heat and let cool completely.
2. Preheat oven to 350°F. Butter two 7-inch loaf pans and dust with flour; tap out excess.
3. With a wooden spoon, stir flour, baking soda, pumpkin pie or Mixed Spice, salt, and egg into marmalade mixture. Transfer mixture to prepared pans and bake for 55 to 60 minutes, or until top is golden and a skewer inserted into center comes out clean.
4. Remove from oven and let cool in pan on a wire rack for 5 minutes. Invert breads onto rack, return to upright, and let cool completely before cutting into slices. Serve spread with butter, if desired.

Note: To make Mixed Spice, in a small bowl, combine, 1 tbsp. ground allspice, 1 tbsp. ground cinnamon, 1 tbsp. ground nutmeg, 2 tsp. ground mace, 1 tsp. ground cloves, 1 tsp. ground coriander, and 1 tsp. ground ginger. Stir to blend; store in a sealed jar.

QUAY HOUSE TEA BRACK

Makes 2 loaves

My first taste of tea brack was at the Quay House, a lovely country house hotel in Clifden, County Galway. Upon arrival, hostess Julia Foyle offers her guests a cup of tea and a slice of this classic Irish loaf made with tea-soaked fruit. Similar in flavor and texture to Scottish, Welsh, and English fruit breads, her recipe includes a healthy portion of nuts and a hint of spice.

- 1 pound mixed dried fruit (such as sultanas, dates, apricots, cranberries), chopped
- 2 tbsp. candied orange peel
- 1/4 cup chopped walnuts
- 1/4 cup chopped pecans
- 1 tsp. ground ginger
- 1 tsp. pumpkin pie spice or Mixed Spice (pg. 61)
- 1 1/4 cups brewed hot tea
- 1 large egg, beaten
- 1 cup (packed) light brown sugar
- 2 cups self-rising flour
- Softened butter, for serving

1. In a large bowl, combine fruit, peel, nuts, ginger, spice, and tea. Let soak for 3 hours, or until tea is absorbed.
2. Preheat oven to 350°F. Butter two 7-inch loaf pans and dust with flour; tap out excess.
3. With a wooden spoon, stir egg, sugar, and flour into fruit mixture; mix until well combined. Transfer mixture to prepared pans and bake for 65 to 70 minutes, or until top is golden and a skewer inserted into center comes out clean.
4. Remove from oven and let cool in pan on a wire rack for 10 minutes. Invert breads onto rack, return to upright, and let cool completely before cutting into slices. Serve spread with butter, if desired.

EARL GREY TEA BRACK

Makes 2 loaves

IN this recipe for tea brack, the fruit is boiled in butter and Earl Grey tea before being mixed with the dry ingredients. The citrus and bergamot flavors of the tea provide a lovely fresh taste.

- 4 oz. unsalted butter, cut into pieces
- 1 cup (packed) light brown sugar
- 1 1/4 cups water
- 2 Earl Grey tea bags
- 1 cup currants
- 1 cup golden raisins
- 3 cups flour
- 1 tsp. baking soda
- 1 tsp. pumpkin pie or Mixed Spice (pg. 61)
- 1 large egg, beaten
- 1 tbsp. apricot jam mixed with 1 tbsp. water, for glaze
- Softened butter, for serving

1. Preheat oven to 300°F. Butter two 7-inch loaf pans and dust with flour; tap out excess.
2. In a large saucepan over medium heat, bring butter, sugar, water, tea bags, currants, and raisins to boil; stir well and cook for 3 to 4 minutes. Remove from heat and let cool for 15 to 20 minutes; discard tea bags.
3. In a medium bowl, whisk together flour, baking soda, and pumpkin pie or Mixed Spice. With a wooden spoon, stir into fruit mixture and then stir in egg.
4. Transfer mixture to prepared pans and bake for 60 to 75 minutes, or until a skewer inserted into center comes out clean. Remove from oven and let cool in pan on a wire rack for 20 minutes. Invert breads onto rack and then return to upright.
5. In a small bowl, heat jam and water in a microwave oven on HIGH for 20 to 25 seconds, or until runny. Brush over top of warm cake; let cool completely before cutting into slices. Serve spread with butter.

Margaret M. Johnson

Manyakotic | Dreamstime.com

APRICOT-WALNUT TEA LOAF

Makes 2 loaves

THIS fruity loaf is a riff on tea brack. Instead of tea, water plumps up the apricots and raisins and both white and wheat flour give it a lovely texture. If you wish, spread the top with apricot jam for added sweetness.

- 1 1/2 cups chopped dried apricots
- 1 cup chopped golden raisins
- 1 1/2 cups boiling water
- 1 oz. butter, at room temperature
- 1 1/3 cup sugar
- 1 large egg
- 1 1/2 cups all-purpose flour
- 1 1/2 cups whole wheat flour
- 2 tsp. baking soda
- 1/2 tsp. salt
- 1/4 tsp. nutmeg
- 1/4 tsp. cinnamon
- 1 cup chopped walnuts
- 1 tbsp. apricot jam mixed with 1 tbsp. water, for glaze (optional)
- Softened butter, for serving

1. Preheat oven to 325°F. Butter two 7-inch loaf pans and dust with flour; tap out excess.
2. In a medium bowl, combine apricots, raisins, and water; let sit for 10 minutes.
3. In a large bowl, beat butter and sugar with an electric mixer on medium speed until light and fluffy; beat in egg. With a wooden spoon, stir in flours, soda, salt, nutmeg, and cinnamon, alternating with apricot mixture; stir in walnuts.
4. Transfer mixture to prepared pans and bake for 65 to 70 minutes, or until top is golden and a skewer inserted into center comes out clean. Remove from oven and let cool on a wire rack for 15 minutes. Invert breads onto rack and then return to upright.
5. In a small bowl, heat apricot jam and water in a microwave on HIGH for 20 to 25 seconds, or until runny; brush over top of warm cake. Let cool completely before cutting into slices. Serve spread with butter, if desired.

APPLE-BRANDY TEA BREAD

Makes 2 loaves

THINK of this recipe for apple bread as a smaller, less-sweet version of traditional Irish apple cake. Although we tend to think of apples as an autumn fruit, this bread is delicious year-round.

- 2 cups flour
- 1 1/2 tsp. salt
- 1 tsp. baking powder
- 1/2 tsp. nutmeg
- 1/2 tsp. ground cinnamon
- 2 cups sugar
- 2 large eggs
- 1/4 cup canola oil
- 2 tbsp. brandy
- 2 Granny Smith apples, peeled, cored, and diced
- 1/4 cup chopped walnuts (optional)
- Softened butter, for serving (optional)

1. Preheat oven to 350° F. Butter two 7-inch loaf pans and dust with flour; tap out excess.
2. In a large bowl, whisk together flour, salt, baking powder, nutmeg, and cinnamon.
3. In a large bowl, beat sugar, eggs, oil, and brandy with an electric mixer on medium speed for 2 to 3 minutes, or until blended. With a wooden spoon, stir into flour mixture until combined. Stir in apples and nuts, if using.
4. Transfer mixture to prepared pans and bake for 50 to 55 minutes, or until a skewer inserted into center comes out clean. Remove from oven and let cool on a wire rack for 10 minutes. Invert breads onto rack, return to upright, and let cool completely before cutting into slices. Serve spread with butter, if desired.

GUINNESS PORTER CAKE

Makes 2 loaves

Even though it's called a cake, this dense, dark bread will often show up at teatime alongside scones and other not-too-sweet fruit breads and bracks. Traditionally served on St. Patrick's Day or for Christmas, it improves with age and can be stored well-wrapped for up to two weeks.

- 4 cups flour
- 1/2 tsp. baking soda
- 1/2 tsp. pumpkin pie spice or Mixed Spice (pg. 61)
- 1/2 tsp. cinnamon
- 8 oz. butter, at room temperature
- 1 cup sugar
- 3 large eggs
- 1 pound mixed dried fruit (such as golden raisins, dates, and currants), chopped
- 1 1/2 cups raisins
- 2/3 cup mixed peel
- 1/2 cup chopped almonds
- 12 oz. Guinness

1. Preheat oven to 300° F. Butter two 7-inch loaf pans and dust with flour; tap out excess.
2. In a large bowl, sift together flour, baking soda, pumpkin pie or Mixed Spice, and cinnamon.
3. In a separate large bowl, beat butter and sugar with an electric mixer on medium speed until light and fluffy. Add eggs, one at a time, beating well after each addition.
4. With a wooden spoon, stir in flour mixture, mixed fruit, raisins, mixed peel, and almonds until blended; stir in Guinness.
5. Transfer mixture to prepared pans and bake for 1 1/2 to 1 3/4 hours, or until a skewer inserted into center comes out clean.
6. Remove from oven and let cool on a wire rack for 10 minutes. Invert loaves onto rack, return upright, and let cool completely before cutting into slices.

Natalia Mylova | Dreamstime.com

The Merrion Hotel

BANANA BREAD

Makes 2 loaves

THE Merrion, originally built for wealthy Irish merchants as four Georgian townhouses in the 1760s, is one of Dublin's most luxurious hotels. After extensive restoration and preservation of the listed buildings, it opened as a luxurious five-star hotel in 1997. Chef Ed Cooney has been in charge of dining operations ever since, and along with a talented and creative team of pastry chefs headed by Paul Kelly, they created an afternoon tea menu that's a genuine "event" for residents and visitors alike. Simply called The Art Tea, it's a clever, sophisticated way to incorporate the hotel's impressive art collection into pastries served at its afternoon tea (pg. 121). One of the less-challenging baking options from The Merrion kitchen is this rich banana bread glazed with warm apricot jam.

- 2 large ripe bananas
- 1 1/4 cups sugar
- 2 1/2 cups flour
- 2 tsp. baking soda
- Pinch of salt
- 2 large eggs
- 3/4 cup milk
- 2/3 cup canola oil
- 2 to 3 tbsp. apricot jam, for glazing
- Softened butter, for serving

1. Preheat oven to 325°F. Butter two 7-inch loaf pans and dust with flour; tap out excess.
2. In a large bowl, beat bananas and sugar with an electric mixer on slow speed for 4 to 5 minutes, or until smooth.
3. In a medium bowl, sift together flour, baking soda and salt.
4. In a small bowl, whisk together eggs and milk.
5. Beat half of flour mixture into banana mixture, alternating with half the eggs mixture; repeat with remaining flour and eggs, scraping down bowl as needed. Stir in oil.
6. Transfer mixture to prepared pans and bake for 50 to 55 minutes, or until top is golden and a skewer inserted into center comes out clean. Remove from oven and let cool on a wire rack for 5 minutes. Invert breads onto rack and then return to upright.
7. In a small bowl, heat jam in a microwave oven on HIGH for 20 to 25 seconds, or until runny. Brush over top of warm cake; let cool completely before cutting into slices. Serve spread with butter, if desired.

Photomailbox | Dreamstime.com

TEATIME FRUITCAKE

Makes 1 loaf

ONE of Ireland's finest hotels, Dromoland Castle in County Clare is among the few castles that can trace its ownership back through history to Irish families of royal heritage. The castle offers luxurious accommodations, elegant dining, and the chance to experience "living like landed gentry" amid the breathtaking scenery of the Clare countryside. Mrs. White's Afternoon Tea, named for a long-standing staff member, is an integral part of the castle experience and the perfect way to unwind after golfing, fishing, or riding on the castle's vast estate. This signature fruit cake will be a delicious addition to your own teatime but be sure to start it at least two days before you want to serve it to let the fruits soak and the flavors meld.

- 1 cup water
- 1 cup raisins
- 1 cup sultanas (golden raisins)
- 2 oz. candied red cherries
- 1 1/2 tbsp. dark rum
- 1 1/2 tbsp. sherry
- 1 tsp. vanilla extract
- 4 oz. unsalted butter, at room temperature
- 1/2 cup sugar
- 2 large eggs
- 1 cup self-rising flour
- 1 teaspoon pumpkin pie spice or Mixed Spice (pg. 61)
- Softened butter, for serving (optional)

1. On the day before baking, in a medium saucepan over medium heat, bring water to boil. Stir in raisins, golden raisins, and cherries; cook for 2 to 3 minutes. Drain fruit and transfer to a small bowl. Stir in rum, sherry, and vanilla extract; cover and let stand overnight.
2. Preheat oven to 300°F. Butter a 9-inch loaf pan and dust with flour; tap out excess.
3. In a large bowl, beat butter and sugar with an electric mixer on medium speed until light and fluffy. Beat in eggs, one at a time, beating well after each addition. With a wooden spoon, fold in the flour and pumpkin pie or Mixed Spice; stir in fruit mixture.
4. Transfer to prepared pan and bake for 60 to 75 minutes, or until a skewer inserted into center comes out clean. Remove from oven and let cool completely on a wire rack. Invert cake onto rack, return to upright, and wrap in aluminum foil; leave overnight before cutting into slices. Serve spread with butter, if desired.

Anjelagr | Dreamstime.com

RASPBERRY-LEMON TEA LOAF

Makes 1 loaf

Serve this sweet-tart tea loaf when raspberries are in season, or switch to blackberries, blueberries, even cranberries when they're available. Like other tea breads and loaves, the glaze or drizzle is optional.

FOR THE LOAF

- 1 cup flour
- 2 tsp. baking powder
- Pinch of salt
- 4 oz. butter, at room temperature
- 1 cup sugar
- Grated zest of 1 lemon
- 2 large eggs
- 1/2 cup plain yogurt
- 2 tbsp. almond flour
- 8 oz. raspberries

FOR THE GLAZE

- 1/2 cup granulated sugar
- Juice of 1 lemon

1. Preheat oven to 350°F. Butter a 9-inch loaf pan and line with parchment paper.
2. In a medium bowl, sift together flour, baking powder, and salt.
3. In a large bowl, beat butter and sugar with an electric mixer on medium speed until light and fluffy; beat in zest. Beat in eggs, one at a time, alternating with flour mixture; beat in yogurt until smooth. Fold in almond flour.
4. Transfer half of mixture to prepared pan and sprinkle over half of the raspberries. Repeat with remaining mixture, ending with raspberries.
5. Bake for 45 to 50 minutes, or until cake is lightly browned. Cover loosely with aluminum foil and bake for 20 to 25 minutes longer, or until a skewer inserted into center comes out clean.
6. Remove cake from oven and let cool on a wire rack for 5 minutes. Invert cake onto rack, remove parchment paper, and then return to upright.
7. Make glaze. Whisk together sugar and lemon juice and spoon it over top of loaf; let soak for 15 minutes before cutting into slices.

Viktorja Puke | Dreamstime.com

ORANGE TEA LOAF

Makes 1 loaf

THIS not-too-sweet tea loaf comes together in a matter of minutes. You can serve it unadorned, tart it up a bit with marmalade glaze, or make it sweeter with a drizzle made with confectioners' sugar and orange juice similar to the glaze recipe on page 77. If you choose to sweeten with the glaze, you might also like to add some candied orange slices (pg. 100).

- 1/2 cup plain yogurt
- 1/2 cup sugar
- 1/2 cup sunflower oil
- 2 large eggs
- 1 1/2 cups self-rising flour
- 1/3 cup fresh orange juice
- 1 tbsp. orange zest
- 1 tbsp. orange marmalade mixed with 1 tbsp. water, for glazing

1. Preheat oven to 300° F. Butter a 9-inch loaf pan and dust with flour; tap out excess.
2. In a large bowl, whisk together yogurt, sugar, oil, and eggs. With a wooden spoon, fold in flour and then stir in orange juice and zest.
3. Transfer mixture to prepared pan and bake for 1 hour, or until a skewer inserted into center comes out clean. Remove from oven and let cool on a wire rack for 5 minutes. Invert cake onto rack and then return to upright.
4. In a small bowl, heat marmalade and water in a microwave on HIGH for 20 to 25 seconds, or until runny; brush marmalade over top of warm cake. Let cool completely before cutting into slices.

Sally Scott | Dreamstime.com

LEMON POPPY SEED TEA BREAD

Makes 1 loaf

C HEF Noel McMeel's food philosophy, whether cooking for friends at home or overseeing the kitchen at Lough Erne Resort in Fermanagh, is based on simplicity. But "simple needn't be bland or boring," he says, and offers this lovely tea bread with flavors of earthy poppy seed and tart lemon as an example. Serve it with scones and tea breads, but if you'd like to add it to the sweets course, you can cut the bread into cubes, pop them into dessert glasses, and drizzle with lemon curd and shaved dark chocolate.

FOR THE BREAD

- 1 1/2 cups flour
- 1 1/4 cups sugar
- 3/4 tsp. salt
- 3/4 tsp. baking powder
- 1 tbsp. poppy seeds
- 1 large egg, beaten
- 2/3 cup canola oil
- 3/4 cup milk
- 1/4 tsp. almond extract
- 1 tsp. vanilla extract

FOR THE GLAZE

- 1 cup confectioners' sugar, sifted
- Juice of 1 lemon
- 1 tbsp. melted butter
- 1/4 tsp. vanilla extract

1. Make bread. Preheat oven to 350° F. Butter a 9-inch loaf pan and dust with flour; tap out excess.
2. In a large bowl, whisk together flour, sugar, salt, baking powder, and poppy seeds. Add egg, oil, milk, almond and vanilla extracts; beat with an electric mixer on medium speed for about 2 minutes, or until blended.
3. Transfer mixture to prepared pan and bake for about 1 hour, or until a skewer inserted into center comes out clean. Remove from oven and let cool on a wire rack for 5 minutes. Invert cake onto rack and then return to upright.
4. Make glaze. In a medium bowl, whisk together sugar, lemon juice, butter, and vanilla until smooth; pour over warm bread. Let cool completely before cutting into slices.

Manyakotic | Dreamstime.com

MIXED BERRY CRUMBLE BARS

Makes 24

Home cooks love a good tray bake, not only for teatime but also for school lunches and picnics. This one has a tasty bottom crust thanks to oats and ground almonds, a lovely filling thanks to fresh berries, and a crunchy topping featuring coconut and more almonds.

- 2 cups flour
- 1 1/2 cups rolled oats
- 1/2 cup (packed) light brown sugar
- 1/2 cup ground almonds
- 1 tsp. baking powder
- 8 oz. unsalted butter, melted
- 4 cups mixed berries
- 2 tbsp. fresh lemon juice
- 1/2 cup granulated sugar
- 2 tbsp. cornstarch
- 1/2 cup flaked almonds
- 1/2 cup shredded coconut

1. Preheat oven to 350°F. Line a 9 x 13-inch pan with parchment paper; coat paper with nonstick cooking spray.
2. In a large bowl, combine flour, oats, brown sugar, ground almonds, and baking powder; stir in butter until blended. Press half of mixture evenly onto bottom of prepared pan.
3. In a large bowl, toss berries with lemon juice. Sprinkle with sugar and cornstarch; toss again until well coated. Spread berries evenly over bottom crust. Stir almonds and coconut into remaining half of crumble mixture and sprinkle over berries.
4. Bake for 50 to 55 minutes, or until the filling is bubbling and the crumble is browned. Remove from oven and let cool on a wire rack for 20 minutes; refrigerate for 1 hour before cutting into 6 rows by 4 rows.

Margaret M. Johnson

GUINNESS APPLESAUCE SLICES

Makes 24

THIS recipe originated with the brewers of Guinness more than four decades ago. A friend made it for me during one of my first visits to Ireland and it remains a favorite. Reminiscent of a holiday spice cake, it's delicious with lemon drizzle or a simple dusting of confectioners' sugar.

FOR THE CAKE

- 1 3/4 cups flour
- 1 tsp. baking soda
- 1/2 tsp. salt
- 1/2 tsp. ground cloves
- 1 tsp. ground cinnamon
- 1 cup unsweetened applesauce
- 3/4 cup (packed) light brown sugar
- 1/2 cup canola oil
- 1/3 cup Guinness
- 1/2 cup sultanas (golden raisins)
- 1/2 cup chopped dates
- 1/2 cup chopped walnuts

FOR THE LEMON DRIZZLE

- 1 1/4 cup confectioners' sugar
- 3 tbsp. milk
- 1 tsp. fresh lemon juice

1. Make cake. Preheat oven to 350° F. Butter a 9 x 13-inch pan.
2. In a large bowl, sift together flour, baking soda, salt, cloves, and cinnamon.
3. In another large bowl, whisk together applesauce, brown sugar, oil, and Guinness; mix well. With a wooden spoon, stir in flour mixture, a little at a time, stirring well after each addition; stir in raisins, dates, and walnuts.
4. Transfer mixture to prepared pan and bake for 30 minutes, or until a skewer inserted in center comes out clean. Remove from oven and let cool on a wire rack for 20 minutes.
5. Make drizzle. In a medium bowl, whisk together sugar, milk, and lemon juice; drizzle mixture over bars. Refrigerate for 1 hour before cutting into 6 rows by 4 rows.

Anjelagr | Dreamstime.com

RASPBERRY-RHUBARB TRAY BAKE

Makes 24

If you travel to Ireland in spring, you're bound to encounter fresh rhubarb—in a pie, tart, muffin, or a tray bake like this. As a true harbinger of the season (although it freezes well and can be used all year), rhubarb's tart taste needs a sweet counterpart, most often strawberries or raspberries. Like the Mixed Berry Crumble Bars on page 79, this recipe uses some of the crust mix on the bottom and some of it for a crunchy topping.

FOR THE CRUST

- 2 1/4 cups flour
- 1 cup granulated sugar
- 1 tsp. baking powder
- 1/4 tsp. salt
- 6 oz. unsalted butter, melted
- 1 large egg yolk, beaten

FOR THE FILLING

- 2 cups raspberries
- 2 cups chopped rhubarb
- 2 tbsp. fresh lemon juice
- 3 tsp. cornstarch

1. Make crust. Preheat oven to 350°F. Line a 9 x 13-inch pan with parchment paper; coat paper with nonstick cooking spray.
2. In a large bowl, whisk together flour, 3/4 cup of sugar, baking powder, and salt. With a pastry cutter or your fingertips, cut or work in butter until mixture resembles coarse crumbs; stir in egg to blend. Gently press half of mixture into prepared pan.
3. Make filling. In a medium bowl, toss raspberries and rhubarb with lemon juice. Sprinkle with remaining 1/4 cup sugar and corn starch; toss again until well coated. Spread raspberries and rhubarb evenly over bottom crust. Sprinkle remaining crumble mixture on top.
4. Bake for 35 to 40 minutes, or until filling is bubbling and crumble is brown. Remove from oven and let cool on wire rack for 20 minutes; refrigerate for 1 hour before cutting into 6 rows by 4 rows.

Margaret M. Johnson

BAKEWELL SLICES

Makes 24

THE original Bakewell Tart is a popular three-part confection consisting of short crust pastry spread with raspberry jam and topped with almond filling. The tart is a variation of the pudding that originated in the English town of Bakewell, and these cakelike slices are a further interpretation. You'll find these slices in bakeries throughout Ireland and the tarts (pg. 101) are often part of a formal afternoon tea.

FOR THE CRUST
- 1 1/2 cups flour
- 3 oz. butter, cut into pieces
- 3 to 4 tbsp. cold water
- 4 tbsp. raspberry jam

FOR THE FILLING
- 4 oz. butter, at room temperature
- 1/2 cup sugar
- 2 large eggs
- 1 cup self-rising flour
- 1/2 cup almond flour
- 1 tsp. baking powder
- 2 tbsp. milk
- 1/2 tsp. almond extract
- Slivered almonds, for topping

1. Make crust. Preheat oven to 350°F. Coat an 8 x 12-inch pan with nonstick cooking spray.
2. Sift flour into a medium bowl. With a pastry cutter or your fingertips, cut or work in butter until mixture resembles coarse crumbs; stir in enough water to make a soft dough.
3. On a floured work surface, roll out dough to fit prepared pan; spread jam over top of crust.
4. Make filling. In a large bowl, beat butter and sugar with an electric mixer on medium speed until light and fluffy. Beat in eggs, one at a time, beating well after each addition. Beat in flours, baking powder, milk, and almond extract until blended. With an offset spatula, spread mixture over raspberry jam; sprinkle with almonds.
5. Bake for 25 to 28 minutes, or until cake is golden and springs back when pressed with your fingertips. Remove from oven and let cool completely on a wire rack before cutting into 6 rows by 4 rows.

TITANIC HOTEL, BELFAST, Northern Ireland Tourist Board

FIFTEENS

Makes 15

FIFTEENS ARE a type of tray bake or "wee bun" popular in Northern Ireland. The name comes from a recipe that calls for fifteen of each of the main ingredients—digestive biscuits, marshmallows, and candied cherries—that are bound together with condensed milk and then rolled in shredded coconut. Slices are traditionally served in Ulster homes with a cup of tea, and at the new Titanic Hotel in Belfast they're frequently offered as part of the afternoon tea service. The hotel, located in the heart of the "Titanic Quarter," was built on the site of the former Harland & Wolff headquarters where the world's most famous ship was designed and built.

- 15 digestive biscuits, such as McVitie's or Carr's brand
- 15 marshmallows, cut into quarters
- 15 candied cherries, cut in half
- 3/4 to 1 cup sweetened condensed milk
- 1/2 to 3/4 cup finely shredded coconut

1. Place biscuits in a food processor or resealable plastic bag; pulse or crush until mixture resembles fine crumbs. Transfer to a large bowl; stir in marshmallows and cherries.
2. Stir in 3/4 cup milk until well combined; add additional milk if needed to make a sticky dough.
3. Sprinkle coconut over a large piece of plastic wrap. Form crumbs mixture into a 2 x 5-inch-long sausage shape and roll in coconut. Wrap plastic tightly around, twisting ends together. Transfer to refrigerator and let chill for 4 to 6 hours, or until firm; cut into 15 slices. Can be stored, wrapped, in refrigerator for up to 1 week.

Isabel Poulin | Dreamstime.com

CHAPTER FOUR

TEATIME SWEETS

I have the simplest of tastes; I am always satisfied with the best.

OSCAR WILDE, IRISH PLAYWRIGHT

The final course in a formal afternoon tea service is, without question, the *pièce de résistance*. Sometimes simply called the "sweets" course, a selection of elegant pastries, cakes, and tarts is anything but simple, with luxurious macarons and heavenly meringues offered alongside more traditional sweets like carrot cake, chocolate brownies, and creamy possets. The sweets course is where pastry chefs really shine and where home cooks—with some kitchen "assistance" from prepared ingredients like frozen puff pastry and sweet tart shells—can bake like a pro.

If meringues, éclairs, or fruit tarts have been absent from your teatime repertoire, fear not! You'll be pleasantly surprised to see how simple it is to recreate ones similar to those served at some of Ireland's most elegant rooms. To put the "wow" factor into your afternoon tea, you can dazzle your guests with Battenberg Cake, a distinctive pink and yellow checked cake covered in fondant; with a painterly posset or parfait like those served at Ashford Castle or Adare Manor; or with a luscious caramel-chocolate-topped confection known as Millionaire's Shortbread. Victoria Sponge, a light, jam-filled layer cake named for the English queen who visited Ireland four times during her reign, plain and simple cupcakes, and tiny pistachio teacakes are other offerings on the sweets course that you can look forward to making and serving.

When Christmas rolls around, most tea rooms offer celebratory holiday-themed teas with mincemeat tarts, gingerbread, and spicy fruit cakes taking pride of place on the top tier, and they're obligatory for teatime at home. And what better excuse than Christmas to put the kettle on and invite friends for tea. For a year-round festive touch, add a glass of champagne, a lovely accompaniment to any teatime experience.

LEMON CREAM TARTLETS

Makes 32

Lemon tarts topped with fresh berries are a delicious, nearly obligatory, addition to teatime and they're simple to make with a no-bake filling and ready-to-fill sweet butter tarts. The optional chocolate lining adds an element of surprise to the tarts, and the pistachio topping is the perfect counterpoint to the silkiness of the lemon cream.

FOR THE FILLING

- 4 large egg yolks
- 1/2 cup sugar
- 1 cup milk
- 1 tbsp. unflavored gelatine
- Grated zest and juice of 1 lemon
- 1 cup heavy (whipping) cream
- 2 oz. dark chocolate, melted (optional)
- 2 packages (1 3/4-inch) butter tarts, such as Clearbrook Farms brand

FOR THE TOPPING

- Fresh berries
- Finely chopped pistachios

1. Make filling. In a medium bowl, beat egg yolks and 1/4 cup of sugar with an electric mixer on medium speed until pale and thick. In a small saucepan over medium heat, bring milk, remaining 1/4 cup sugar, and gelatine to a boil. Gradually whisk milk mixture into yolk mixture.
2. Return to saucepan and cook, stirring constantly, for 3 to 5 minutes, or until bubbles form around edges of pan. Strain mixture through a fine-mesh sieve into a bowl, stir in lemon zest and juice, and press a piece of plastic wrap directly onto surface to prevent a skin from forming. Refrigerate for 18 to 20 minutes, or until mixture thickens.
3. In a small bowl, whip cream with an electric mixer on high speed until soft peaks form; fold into lemon mixture.
4. With a pastry brush, coat inside of pastry shells with a thin layer of chocolate, if using; allow to cool and set. Spoon lemon cream into each tart shell and refrigerate for 15 minutes.
5. Arrange berries on top and sprinkle with pistachios.

VICTORIA SPONGE

Serves 8 to 10

This traditional cake—some say it's the "quintessential teatime sweet"—consists of jam and whipped cream sandwiched between two sponge cakes. The top of the cake is generally not iced or decorated except for a sprinkling of confectioners' sugar, sometimes over a doily to create a lacy pattern. The cake is named in honor of Queen Victoria, who spent time at her residence on the Isle of Wight following the death of Prince Albert in 1861. In order to inspire the monarch to resume some of her civic duties, she was encouraged to host tea parties, at which a sponge cake like this was served. "Victoria Sponges" became fashionable throughout England and Ireland and the measure of a home baker. This recipe is from the tearoom at Belleek, Ireland's oldest working fine china company, which was established in 1857 in the village of Belleek, County Fermanagh, on the banks of the River Erne.

FOR THE CAKE

- 6 oz. butter
- 3/4 cup sugar
- 4 large eggs, beaten
- 2 cups self-rising flour
- 1 tsp. baking powder

FOR THE FILLING

- 1/2 cup strawberry or raspberry jam
- 2/3 cup heavy cream, whipped
- Confectioners' sugar, for dusting
- Fresh strawberries, for garnish (optional)

1. Make cake. Preheat oven to 325° F. Butter a 9-inch round pan and dust with flour; tap out excess.
2. In a medium bowl, beat butter and sugar with an electric mixer on medium speed until light and fluffy. Add eggs one at a time, beating well after each addition. Whisk in flour and baking powder until smooth.
3. Transfer mixture to prepared pan and bake for 30 to 35 minutes, or until the top is golden and a skewer inserted into the center comes out clean. Remove cake from oven and let cool on a wire rack for 15 minutes,
4. Invert cake onto a serving plate, and then return it to upright. With a serrated knife, cut the cake in half horizontally; spread the bottom half with strawberry or raspberry jam. Spread whipped cream over jam and replace top half of cake.
5. Place a 9-inch doily on top of the cake and lightly sift confectioners' sugar over it. Carefully remove doily, leaving a lacy pattern on cake. Cover and refrigerate cake until serving time. Garnish with fresh strawberries, if desired.

Belleek Pottery

COURGETTE AND LIME CAKELETS

Makes 40

LEMONY Lemon Drop tea is a refreshing mélange of rooibos (South African red bush tea), lemongrass, and marigold petals artfully blended by Alison McArdle for her Cupán Tae shops/cafés in Galway and Westport, County Mayo. In this recipe, one of many of tea-infused foods she serves for afternoon tea, the subtle citrus notes in the tea provide a unique flavor to an otherwise simple courgette (zucchini) cake. You can slice and fill the cakelets with lime curd and top with matcha cream cheese icing or spread the icing on top and put a dollop of lime curd in the center. Either way, these little cakes make a real statement. To make your own version of Lemony Lemon Drop tea, add some Lady Grey tea to rooibos.

FOR THE CAKELETS

- 5 tsp. Lemony Lemon Drops tea, or a rooibos blend
- 3/4 cup boiling water
- 1 cup raisins
- 3 large eggs
- 1 cup sunflower oil
- 1 2/3 cups sugar
- 3 cups flour
- 1 tsp. baking powder
- 1 tsp. baking soda
- 1 tsp. salt
- 2 cups grated courgettes, squeezed to remove excess moisture

FOR THE LIME CURD

- 3 large eggs
- 1 cup sugar
- 4 oz. cold butter, cut into pieces
- 1/2 cup fresh lime juice

FOR THE ICING

- 4 oz. cream cheese, at room temperature
- 4 oz. butter, at room temperature
- 2 cups confectioners' sugar
- 1 tsp. matcha green tea

1. Make cakes. In a small bowl, combine tea, water, and raisins; soak for 30 minutes. Strain; reserve tea and raisins.
2. Preheat oven to 325°F. Coat two mini fluted cupcake pans with cooking oil spray.
3. In a medium bowl, beat eggs, oil, sugar, and reserved tea with an electric mixer on medium speed for 2 to 3 minutes, or until smooth.
4. In a medium bowl, whisk together flour, baking powder, baking soda, and salt. Beat flour mixture into eggs mixture in three additions; stir in raisins and courgettes.
5. Spoon or scoop mixture into prepared pans, filling halfway full. Bake for 15 to 17 minutes, or until a skewer inserted into center comes out clean. Repeat with remaining mixture.
6. Make curd. In top of double boiler set over simmering water, whisk eggs until frothy. Stir in sugar until blended; add butter and lime juice.
7. Cook over medium heat, stirring constantly, for 15 to 20 minutes, or until mixture thickens and coats back of a spoon. Pour into 2 small jars; cool to room temperature. Cover and refrigerate for up to 1 week.
8. Make icing. In a large bowl, beat cream cheese and butter with an electric mixer on medium speed until blended. Gradually beat in confectioners' sugar and tea until smooth. Transfer to a piping bag fitted with a large open-star tip and decoratively pipe onto cakes. Refrigerate for 1 hour.

Bewley's

CARROT CAKE

Serves 8

If you think carrot cake is an American classic, you'll be surprised to find it in one shape or another on afternoon tea menus throughout Ireland: in a small round with an orange cream center, in a mini cheesecake, and in this triple-layer stack with cream cheese filling at Bewley's Grafton Street Café, Dublin. The patisserie chefs there add a thin layer of carrot and orange sauce and a chocolate biscuit to the top layer, but a shaving of dark chocolate or the candied orange slices (pg. 100) works equally well.

FOR THE CAKE

- 1 cup sugar
- 2 large eggs
- 1/3 cup canola oil
- 1 1/4 cups flour
- 2 tsp. baking powder
- 1/2 tsp. baking soda
- 1/2 tsp. ground cinnamon
- 1/2 tsp. sea salt
- 8 oz. shredded carrots, chopped
- 1/4 cup chopped macadamia nuts

FOR THE FILLING

- 2 oz. unsalted butter, at room temperature
- 4 oz. cream cheese, at room temperature
- 1/2 tsp. vanilla extract
- Pinch of salt
- 2 cups confectioners' sugar
- 4 oz. dark chocolate, shaved, for garnish
- Candied orange slices, for garnish (optional)

1. Make cake. Preheat the oven to 350°F. Line a 9 x 14-inch rimmed baking sheet with parchment paper.
2. In a large bowl, beat sugar, eggs, and oil with an electric mixer on medium speed for about 3 minutes, or until blended.
3. In a medium bowl, whisk together flour, baking powder, baking soda, cinnamon, and salt. Stir half of flour mixture into oil mixture; stir in remaining flour, carrots and nuts until blended.
4. Transfer mixture to prepared pan and smooth to edges. Bake for 28 to 30 minutes, or until edges are golden and skewer inserted into center comes out clean. Remove from oven and let cool completely in pan on a wire rack.
5. Make filling. In a large bowl, beat butter, cream cheese, vanilla, and salt with an electric mixer on medium speed for 3 to 4 minutes, or until blended. Gradually beat in confectioners' sugar until smooth.
6. To assemble, with an offset spatula, loosen cake from pan. Invert cake onto work surface and remove paper; trim edges. With a serrated knife, cut cake into three 4 1/2 x 9-inch pieces. Spread a thick layer of icing over one slice; repeat with remaining icing and slices to create 3 layers. Garnish with chocolate and orange slices, if using. Refrigerate for 1 hour and then cut into slices.

Ashford Castle

LEMON MERINGUE TARTS

Serves 20

ASHFORD Castle in Cong, County Mayo, is one of Ireland's most famous properties. Once under the ownership of the Guinness family, it will always be associated with their name, especially Lord and Lady Ardilaun, who enjoyed one of the great romances of the time while living here. In celebration of their 25th wedding anniversary, they received a gift of a beautiful silver tea service, still on display at the entrance to the Connaught Room, where guests today enjoy afternoon tea named in their honor. These lemon curd tarts, with a hint of almond in the pastry, are a selection from the sweets course.

FOR THE PASTRY

- 2 cups flour
- 5 oz. cold butter, cut into pieces
- 1/2 cup ground almonds
- 1 cup confectioners' sugar
- 1 large egg
- 1 large egg yolk

FOR THE FILLING

- 3 large eggs
- 1 1/4 cups sugar
- Grated zest from 1/2 lemon
- 1/4 cup fresh lemon juice
- 4 oz. unsalted butter, at room temperature, cut into pieces
- 3 oz. white chocolate
- 1 tsp. cocoa butter
- 1 tsp. gelatine

FOR THE MERINGUE

- 1/4 cup water
- 2 tbsp. liquid glucose or light corn syrup, such as Karo brand
- 1/2 cup sugar
- 2 large egg whites

1. Make pastry. In a food processor, combine flour and butter; pulse until mixture resembles fine bread crumbs. Add confectioners' sugar and almonds. With machine running, slowly add egg and egg yolk until mixture comes together (do not overwork).
2. Gather dough into a disk, wrap in plastic, and refrigerate for 30 minutes.
3. Preheat oven to 325°F. Transfer dough to a floured surface and roll into a 1/4-inch-thick round. With a 3-inch round cookie cutter, cut out 12 rounds. Press rounds into wells of a standard tart pan (or use individual tart molds) and bake blind for 20 to 24 minutes, or until lightly browned. Remove from oven, transfer to a wire rack, and let cool for 5 minutes; remove shells from pan. Reroll dough, cut out additional rounds, and bake as above.
4. Make filling. In a medium saucepan over medium heat, whisk together eggs, sugar, lemon juice, and zest. Cook, stirring constantly, until mixture thickens and temperature on a candy thermometer reaches 200°F.
5. Remove from heat and whisk in butter, white chocolate, cocoa butter, and gelatin. With an immersion blender, blend for at least 5 minutes, or until mixture is light and smooth. Spoon or pipe into tart shells.
6. Make meringue. In a small saucepan over medium heat, combine water, glucose or corn syrup, and 1/3 cup of the sugar. Cook, stirring constantly, until temperature on a candy thermometer reaches 200°F.
7. Beat egg whites and remaining sugar with an electric mixer on high speed. Slowly beat cooked sugar mixture into egg whites until fully incorporated.
8. Transfer meringue mixture into a piping bag fitted with a small nozzle and pipe onto tarts. With a kitchen torch, lightly brown tops.

Dplmborough | Dreamstime.com

BATTENBERG CAKE

Serves 8

BATTENBERG Cake is a light marzipan-covered sponge cake that's made distinctive by its checkerboard design, most often pink and white or pink and yellow. The origin of the name is not clear, but one theory suggests that the cake was created in honor of the marriage in 1884 of Queen Victoria's granddaughter to Prince Louis of Battenberg. The four squares of the cake are said to represent the four Battenberg princes.

- 4 oz. butter, at room temperature
- 3/4 cup superfine sugar
- 2 large eggs
- 1 1/2 cups self-rising flour
- 3 tsp. baking powder
- 1/2 tsp. almond extract
- 1/4 cup milk
- 2 to 3 drops red food coloring
- 1/2 cup apricot jam, heated
- 1 (24-oz.) box white fondant, such as Wilton brand

1. Make cake. Preheat oven to 350°F. Coat an 8-inch square pan with nonstick cooking spray. Line pan with parchment paper and spray again. Cut a piece of cardboard into a 2 x 8-inch rectangle (to serve as a barrier between the two colors). Place in center of pan; cover pan and divider with a 12 x 8-inch piece of parchment paper; spray again.
2. In a large bowl, beat butter and sugar with an electric mixer on medium speed until light and fluffy. Beat in the eggs, one at a time, beating well after each addition. Fold in flour, baking powder, almond extract, and milk.
3. Transfer half of batter to one side of prepared pan. Add food coloring to other half of batter and stir until batter is deep pink in color. Transfer pink batter to other half of pan and smooth tops of both halves; tap pan a few times to remove air bubbles.
4. Bake cake for 25 to 28 minutes, or until a skewer inserted into center comes out clean. Remove from oven and let cool in pan on a wire rack for about 5 minutes. Invert cakes onto rack to cool completely.
5. Cut cakes lengthwise in half to make four equal pieces (approximately 1 1/8 inches wide). Wrap each section in plastic wrap and let stand overnight.
6. Place white piece and pink piece side-by-side on a flat surface and spread tops and center with apricot preserves to "glue" the pieces together. Repeat with remaining pink and white strips to create a checkerboard effect; spread with preserves to adhere pieces. Spread top and sides of cake with remaining jam; trim ends of cake evenly.
7. Make fondant: Knead and roll fondant to an 8 x 10-inch rectangle according to package directions.
8. Place cake, jam-side down, in center of fondant. Wrap cake with fondant; press and smooth to adhere to cake. Turn cake over; fold in ends and smooth. Wrap cake tightly in plastic; chill for about 1 hour.
9. To serve, unwrap cake; trim ends. With a serrated knife, cut cake into 8 slices.

THREE FRUIT MARMALADE CAKE

Serves 8 to 10

CROSSOGUE is an award-winning line of small-batch preserves, chutneys, and marmalades made with interesting ingredients such as plum and orange, blackcurrant and Irish stout, strawberry and Champagne, and three fruit—lemon, orange, and grapefruit—the key ingredient in this lovely tea cake. Spooned into and on top of the cake, the made-in-Tipperary marmalade is, as expected, also delicious spread on toast and scones. For a decorative touch, arrange candied orange slices on top of cake, if you wish.

FOR THE CANDIED ORANGE SLICES

- 2 cups sugar
- 2 cups water
- 12 thin slices from 1 seedless orange

FOR THE CAKE

- 1 cup self-rising flour, sifted
- 1 tsp. baking powder
- 4 oz. butter, at room temperature
- 1/2 cup sugar
- 2 large eggs
- 1 tbsp. hot water
- 5 tbsp. three fruit marmalade

1. Make orange slices. In a medium saucepan over medium heat, bring sugar and water to boil, stirring until sugar dissolves. Reduce heat to low and add orange slices. Cook for about 10 minutes, or until slices are translucent. Remove from heat and let slices cool completely in syrup.
2. Make cake. Preheat oven to 350°F. Butter an 8-inch baking pan and line with parchment paper.
3. In a large bowl, beat flour, butter, sugar, eggs, water, and 3 tablespoons marmalade with an electric mixer on medium speed for 2 to 3 minutes, or until blended.
4. Transfer to prepared pan and bake for 35 to 40 minutes, or until a skewer inserted into center comes out clean. Remove from oven and let cool on a wire rack for 15 minutes. Invert cake onto rack, return to upright, and let cool for 1 hour. Spread remaining 2 tablespoons marmalade over top of cake.
5. If desired, remove orange slices from syrup, cut in half, and arrange decoratively over top of cake.

BAKEWELL TARTS

Makes 24

These little tarts, named for the English town of Bakewell, are made with short crust pastry, raspberry jam, and the almond filling known as frangipane. It originated as a pudding, later became popular as a full-size tart, and can also be baked as slices (pg. 85). Regardless of the shape or size, it's a popular addition to teatime.

FOR THE PASTRY
- 1 cup flour
- 2 tbsp. sugar
- 1/2 tsp. salt
- 3 oz. cold butter, cut into small pieces
- 2 large egg yolks
- 1/2 tsp. vanilla extract
- 1 to 2 tbsp. cold water

FOR THE FILLING
- 1/2 cup raspberry jam
- 4 oz. butter
- 1 cup sugar
- 2 tbsp. grated lemon zest
- 2 large eggs, beaten
- 1/2 cup flour, sifted
- 1/2 cup ground almonds
- 1/4 cup flaked almonds
- Confectioners' sugar, for dusting

1. Make pastry. In a food processor, combine flour, sugar, and salt; pulse 1 to 2 times. Add butter, a few pieces at a time, and pulse until mixture resembles coarse crumbs. Add egg yolks, vanilla, and water; process until dough comes together.
2. Transfer dough to a work surface, form into a ball, and then wrap in plastic wrap and refrigerate for 30 minutes.
3. Preheat oven to 375°F. Coat the cups of a mini cupcake pan with nonstick spray.
4. Dust a work surface with flour. Flatten dough into a disk, cut in half, and then roll out each half to a 1/4-inch-thick round. With a 2-inch cookie cutter, cut out 12 rounds from each half. Fit each into a cup and gently press into cup.
5. Make filling. Put 1 teaspoon of jam into each cup. Combine butter, sugar, and lemon zest in a food processor; process for 20 to 30 seconds, or until light and fluffy. Process eggs, one at a time, and then add flour and almonds; process 10 to 20 seconds, or until well blended.
6. Spoon mixture into pastry-lined cups; sprinkle with almonds. Bake for 23 to 25 minutes, or until golden. Remove from oven and let cool on a wire rack for 10 minutes. Remove tartlets from pan and dust with confectioners' sugar.

PISTACHIO TEA CAKES

Makes 28

Pistachio cake is one of the most popular desserts served in Pygmalion Restaurant, the formal dining room at Parknasilla Resort in Sneem, County Kerry. Nutty, flourless, and moist, the cake is easily transformed into little tea cakes when baked in mini fluted Bundt pans. Serve them simply dusted with confectioners' sugar or top them with pistachio buttercream and sprinkle with finely chopped pistachios, if you wish.

FOR THE CAKES

- 5 oz. almonds
- 3 oz. unsalted pistachios
- 8 oz. butter, at room temperature
- 2 cups sugar
- 3 tbsp. pistachio paste
- 5 large eggs

FOR THE PISTACHIO BUTTERCREAM

- 4 oz. butter, at room temperature
- 4 tbsp. pistachio paste
- 2 cups confectioners' sugar
- 2 tbsp. heavy (whipping) cream
- 1 tsp. vanilla extract
- Finely chopped pistachios, for garnish

1. Make cakes. Preheat oven to 325° F. Coat the cups of 2 mini fluted Bundt pans with nonstick baking spray.
2. In a food processor, combine almonds and pistachios; process for 30 to 40 seconds, or until nuts are finely ground.
3. In a medium bowl, beat butter, sugar, and pistachio paste with an electric mixer on medium speed until light and fluffy. Slowly add ground nuts, alternating with eggs, until mixture is blended and smooth.
4. Spoon mixture into prepared pans, filling half full; let rest for 10 minutes to ensure mixture settles into cups. Bake for 25 to 28 minutes, or until a skewer inserted into center comes out clean. Remove pans from oven and let cool on a wire rack for 10 minutes. Loosen cakes from sides of pan with a small knife; invert onto rack and tap gently to remove cakes. Cool completely. Repeat with remaining mixture.
5. Make buttercream. In a medium bowl, beat butter and pistachio paste with an electric mixer on medium speed for 1 minute; gradually beat in confectioners' sugar, cream, and vanilla until smooth. Drizzle over cakes and sprinkle with nuts.

LEMON POSSET WITH CITRUS JELLY

Makes 8

A "posset" is a creamy old-fashioned drink that's become quite fashionable as part of a formal afternoon tea service. Pudding-like in texture, it adapts well to any number of flavorings—most often citrus—and chefs generally top it with a fruity jelly or compote and present it in 2-ounce cordial glasses. At luxurious Adare Manor in County Limerick, afternoon tea is served in The Gallery, a room with soaring arches and ancient woodwork. Here the lemon posset comes with an exotic topping of sea buckthorn jelly, but a more accessible flavoring is made with orange purée, a delicious condiment made with a whole orange.

FOR THE ORANGE PURÉE
- 1 large seedless orange
- 3 cups sugar
- 3 cups water

FOR THE POSSET
- 2 cups heavy (whipping) cream
- 1/4 cup sugar
- Zest and juice from 2 lemons

FOR THE JELLY
- 1 cup orange purée
- 1/3 cup sugar
- 1 tbsp. gelatine

Adare Manor

1. Make purée. With the tip of a sharp knife, cut 5 to 6 slits in orange skin. In a medium saucepan over medium-high heat, bring sugar and water to a boil, stirring until sugar is dissolved. Reduce heat to medium-low, add orange, and cook, stirring frequently, for about 1 hour, or until orange is very tender.
2. Remove from heat and let cool for about 20 minutes. Cut orange in half and then cut into large pieces. Transfer to a food processor or blender with 1 cup of syrup; process for 1 to 2 minutes, or until smooth. Press through a fine mesh strainer, cover, and refrigerate (freeze unused purée).
3. Make posset. In a medium saucepan over medium heat, slowly bring sugar and cream to boil; cook for 3 to 5 minutes, or until slightly thickened. Add juice and zest; return to a medium heat and cook for 2 minutes longer. Remove from heat and fill eight 2-ounce glasses two-thirds full. Let cool for 15 minutes; refrigerate for 8 to 10 hours, or until set.
4. Make jelly. In a small saucepan over medium heat, bring orange purée and sugar to a boil; remove from heat and stir in gelatine until dissolved. Spoon a thin layer over possets; return to refrigerator for 1 to 2 hours, or until set.

WHITE CHOCOLATE-PASSION FRUIT VERRINE

Makes 10

At the Westbury Hotel in Dublin, afternoon tea is served in The Gallery, a luxurious space overlooking Grafton Street. The hotel often presents themed teas, like the recent one partnering with the National College of Art and Design where the kitchen and the college collaborated by featuring handcrafted sweets inspired by fashion techniques practiced at the college. This verrine—the name is for a small glass container used to hold layered hors d'oeuvres or desserts—is a creamy three-part culinary interpretation of a collection influenced by traditional clothing styles from Arranmore, an island off the Donegal coast. Westbury chefs craft the white chocolate into a lacy knit-like pattern, but home cooks can simply spoon the cream on top.

FOR THE CRÉMEUX
- 4 large egg yolks
- 2 tbsp. sugar
- 1/2 cup milk
- 1/2 cup heavy (whipping) cream
- 1/2 tbsp. unflavored gelatine
- 3/4 cups coconut milk, such a Thai brand

FOR THE PASSION FRUIT JELLY
- 1 whole passion fruit or 3 oz. frozen passion fruit, thawed
- 1 tbsp. sugar
- 1/2 tbsp. unflavored gelatine

FOR THE WHITE CHOCOLATE GANACHE
- 2 tbsp. coconut purée or finely ground coconut
- 2 tbsp. coconut milk
- 1/2 tbsp. glucose or corn syrup, such as Karo brand
- 2 oz. white chocolate, melted
- 1/2 cup heavy (whipping) cream
- 1/2 tbsp. Malibu liqueur

1. Make crémeux. In a medium bowl, whisk together egg yolks and half the sugar.
2. In a small saucepan over medium heat, bring milk and cream to a boil. Slowly whisk into egg yolks mixture.

Return mixture to heat, whisk in remaining sugar, and cook, whisking constantly, for 3 to 4 minutes, or until mixture reaches 180°F on a candy thermometer.

3. Remove from heat; cool mixture to about 110°F. Gradually stir in gelatine until dissolved, and then whisk in coconut milk in three additions. With an immersion blender, beat until smooth and emulsified; let cool for about 10 minutes. Transfer to a measuring cup (for ease of pouring) and pour into ten 2-ounce glasses. Refrigerate for 1 hour, or until chilled.

4. Make passion fruit jelly. Cut passion fruit in half and scoop out seeds. Transfer to a food processor or blender and process for 1 to 2 minutes, or until smooth.

5. In a small saucepan over medium heat, bring passion fruit purée and sugar to a boil; remove from heat and stir in gelatine until dissolved. Let cool for 15 minutes, and then spoon over crémeux; return to refrigerator.

6. Make white chocolate ganache. In a small saucepan over medium heat, bring coconut purée or ground coconut, milk, and corn syrup to a boil. Remove from heat; whisk in chocolate and liqueur until smooth; refrigerate for 1 hour. At serving time, whip until soft peaks form and spoon on top.

The Westbury

CASTLEWOOD HOUSE, DINGLE, Margaret M. Johnson

CHOCOLATE-WHISKEY TORTE

Serves 10 to 12

At Castlewood House, an award-winning small hotel in Dingle, County Kerry, super hosts Brian and Helen Heaton treat guests like friends, offering Champagne on arrival and a day-long supply of goodies on a buffet in the sitting room. This torte, with a big bowl of whipped cream alongside—Helen feels the cream balances the dark chocolate and whiskey—is one of the most popular to have with a cup of tea in the afternoon.

- 4 oz. butter
- 8 oz. (70% cocoa solids) dark chocolate
- 1/3 cup granulated sugar
- 1/4 cup flour
- Pinch of salt
- 3 large eggs
- 2 tbsp. Irish whiskey
- 1/4 cup (packed) dark brown sugar
- Whipped cream, for serving

1. Preheat oven to 350°F. Butter an 8-inch springform pan and dust with flour; tap out excess.
2. In a small saucepan over medium heat, melt butter until sizzling. Remove from heat and whisk in chocolate until smooth; let cool.
3. In a medium bowl, whisk together granulated sugar, flour, and salt; whisk in eggs and whiskey until smooth.
4. Stir brown sugar into cooled chocolate mixture and then stir into flour mixture.
5. Transfer to prepared pan and bake for 25 minutes. Remove from oven and let cool on a wire rack for 15 minutes. Release sides of pan and let cake cool completely before cutting into slices. Serve with whipped cream, if desired.

Margaret M. Johnson

CHOCOLATE BROWNIES WITH BURNT WHITE CHOCOLATE CREAM

Makes 12

CELEBRITY chef/television presenter Paula McIntyre MBE shares her culinary skills with a wide audience, including at intimate cooking classes at places like Quilly House in Coleraine, Northern Ireland, the farmhouse of the Kane family, proprietors of the award-winning Broighter Gold rapeseed oil. For a festive accompaniment, serve the brownies with a glass of Champagne!

FOR THE BROWNIES

- 8 oz. dark chocolate, chopped
- 6 oz. butter, cut into pieces
- 3 large eggs
- 1/2 cup muscovado sugar
- 1/2 cup sugar
- 2 tsp. vanilla extract
- 1 cup flour

FOR THE BURNT CREAM

- 4 oz. white chocolate, roughly broken
- 8 oz. mascarpone cheese
- 1 cup heavy (whipping) cream
- 1 tbsp. honey

1. Make brownies. Preheat oven to 350°F. Butter an 8-inch square baking pan.
2. In a small saucepan over medium heat, melt butter and chocolate until smooth; let cool.
3. In a medium bowl, beat eggs and sugars with an electric mixer on medium speed until pale and thick. Fold in chocolate mixture, vanilla, and flour.
4. Transfer to prepared pan and bake for 25 minutes, or until center is still slightly wobbly (brownies should not be firm to touch). Remove from oven and let cool completely on a wire rack before cutting into 12 squares.
5. Reduce oven temperature to 250°F. Line a baking sheet with parchment paper. Scatter chocolate on prepared pan; bake for 1 hour, or until golden. Cool and chop finely.
6. In a small bowl, whisk together mascarpone, cream, and honey; fold in white chocolate. Transfer mixture to a piping bag fitted with a medium open star tip. To serve, pipe an upright rosette onto each brownie.

Margaret M. Johnson

LEMON CURD LAYER CAKE

Serves 8 to 10

AVOCA Cafés and restaurants serve luscious lunches, dreamy confections, and sweet treats to eat in or to take away. Many tea party hosts supplement their own baked goods with offerings from Avoca, like this lemon curd cake, which comes beautifully embellished with seasonal fruits and a glacé icing. If you bake the cake at home, you can use a simple buttercream icing and sprinkle the top with lemon zest; berries are optional.

FOR THE CAKE

- 8 oz. butter, at room temperature
- 1 cup sugar
- 4 large eggs
- 2 cups self-rising flour, sifted
- 1 tsp. baking powder, sifted
- Grated zest of 1 lemon, plus more for topping
- 1 1/2 tbsp. fresh lemon juice
- Lemon curd, for filling (pg. 59 and 97)

FOR THE ICING

- 4 oz. butter, at room temperature
- 1 cup confectioners' sugar
- 2 tsp. fresh lemon juice
- Lemon zest, for sprinkling
- Fresh berries, for garnish (optional)

1. Make cake. Preheat oven to 325°F. Butter a 9-inch springform pan and line with parchment paper.
2. In a large bowl, beat butter and sugar with an electric mixer on medium speed until light and fluffy. Beat in eggs, alternating with flour and baking powder, and then beat in lemon zest and juice.
3. Transfer mixture to prepared pan and bake for 55 to 60 minutes, or until a skewer inserted into center comes out clean. Remove from oven and cool on a wire rack for 15 minutes.
4. Remove sides of pan and let cake cool completely. With a serrated knife, cut the cake in half horizontally and spread the bottom half with lemon curd; replace top half of cake.
5. Make icing. In a medium bowl, beat butter, sugar, and lemon juice with an electric mixer on medium speed until light and fluffy. With an offset spatula, spread icing over sides and top of cake. Sprinkle top with lemon zest; refrigerate for 1 hour before cutting into slices. Decoratively arrange fresh berries on top, if desired.

ORANGE AND POPPY SEED CUPCAKES WITH ORANGE BUTTER-CREAM ICING

Makes 12 cupcakes

Who doesn't love a cupcake? They're easy to make, easy to eat, and make a big splash on the top tier with luscious icings and whimsical decorations. At Titanic Belfast, the popular visitor experience that traces the famous ship from inception to fateful ending, afternoon tea is served every Sunday in the ballroom. The tea menu changes on a seasonal basis and includes cheesecake, macarons, and cupcakes like these. Sprinkle orange zest on top or garnish with a small wedge of candied orange (pg. 100).

FOR THE CUPCAKES

- 1 1/2 cups all-purpose flour
- 1/2 tsp. salt
- 1/4 tsp. baking powder
- 1/4 tsp. baking soda
- 4 oz. butter, at room temperature
- 1 cup sugar
- 2 large eggs
- 2 tsp. grated orange zest
- 1/2 tsp. orange extract
- 1/2 cup buttermilk
- 1 tbsp. poppy seeds

FOR THE ICING

- 4 oz. unsalted butter, at room temperature
- 2 cups confectioners' sugar
- 3 tbsp. milk
- 1/2 tsp. orange extract
- Pinch of salt
- Grated orange zest, for garnish

1. Make cupcakes. Preheat oven to 350°F. Line cups of a standard cupcake pan with paper liners.
2. In a medium bowl, whisk together flour, salt, baking powder and baking soda.
3. In a large bowl, beat butter and sugar with an electric mixer on medium speed until light and fluffy. Add eggs, one at a time, beating well after each addition; stir in orange zest and extract.
4. Gradually add flour mixture to butter mixture, alternating with buttermilk, and beat at low speed until just combined; fold in poppy seeds.
5. Spoon or scoop mixture into prepared pan, filling each cup three quarters full. Bake for 20 to 23 minutes, or until a skewer inserted into center comes out clean. Remove from oven and let cool for 5 minutes. Transfer to a wire rack and let cool completely.
6. Make icing. In a large bowl, beat butter with an electric mixer on medium speed for 1 minute. Beat in confectioners' sugar, milk, orange extract, and salt until smooth. Transfer to a piping bag fitted with a large open-star tip and decoratively pipe onto cupcakes. Refrigerate for 1 hour.

MILLIONAIRE'S SHORTBREAD

Makes 12

SHORTBREAD, which is neither short nor bread, originated in Scotland as a byproduct of the country's abundant dairy industry. In ancient times, butter was combined with oatmeal, another peasant staple, and baked into "short" cakes, so called because of the high butter content that made them very crumbly. In the sixteenth century, shortbread grew more refined as it became popular throughout the United Kingdom and Ireland; in more recent times, the humble shortbread has taken on further refinement with the addition of two luxurious layers of caramel and chocolate in what's come to be known as "Millionaire's Shortbread."

FOR THE SHORTBREAD
- 2 cups flour
- 6 oz. cold butter, cut into pieces
- 1/3 cup sugar

FOR THE CARAMEL TOPPING
- 5 oz. butter
- 1 (13-oz.) can sweetened condensed milk
- 1/2 cup golden syrup, such as Lyle's brand

FOR THE CHOCOLATE TOPPING
- 12 oz. dark chocolate
- 1/2 cup heavy (whipping) cream

1. Preheat oven to 300° F. Line a 9-inch square baking pan with aluminum foil long enough to extend over the sides of the pan; coat foil with nonstick cooking spray.
2. In a food processor, combine flour and butter; pulse 5 to 6 times, or until mixture resembles fine crumbs. Add sugar and pulse again until combined.
3. Transfer mixture to prepared pan and spread evenly. With your fingers, press mixture firmly into pan, spreading to corners. Bake for 30 minutes, or until lightly browned. Remove from oven and let cool on a wire rack.
4. Make caramel. In a medium saucepan over medium heat, combine butter, condensed milk, and golden syrup; stir until butter melts and mixture is smooth. Bring mixture to a boil, stirring frequently, and continue to cook until caramel thickens and browns. Remove from heat; let cool for 10 minutes. Pour over shortbread and spread evenly; let cool completely.
5. In a small saucepan over medium heat, combine chocolate and cream; stir frequently until chocolate melts and mixture is smooth. Remove from heat; let cool for 5 minutes. Pour over caramel and spread evenly; refrigerate for about 30 minutes. Using the foil handles, lift out of pan; cut into 12 squares.

Northern Ireland Tourist Board

ÉCLAIRS

Makes 18 large or 24 mini

ÉCLAIRS are French pastries made with choux pastry and filled with custard or whipped cream. The name comes from the French word for "lightning," and it's believed that the pastry is so-called because it sparkles when coated with a shiny chocolate ganache or other fondant icing. While French in origin, the lovely little pastries are frequently part of a formal Irish afternoon tea, perfectly crafted by pastry chefs but easy enough to make at home. For large éclairs, pipe the dough in 5-inch portions; for mini éclairs, pipe the dough in 3-inch portions.

FOR THE ÉCLAIRS

- 1/2 cup water
- 1/2 cup milk
- 4 oz. butter
- 1/4 tsp. salt
- 1 cup flour
- 4 large eggs

FOR THE PASTRY CREAM

- 2 cups milk
- 1 tsp. vanilla bean paste
- 3/4 cup sugar
- 1/4 cup cornstarch
- Pinch of salt
- 4 large egg yolks
- 2 oz. unsalted butter, cut into small pieces

FOR THE CHOCOLATE TOPPING

- 4 oz. semisweet chocolate
- 1/2 cup heavy (whipping) cream

1. Make éclairs. Preheat oven to 425°F. Line 2 rimmed baking sheets with parchment paper or spray a mini éclair pan with nonstick cooking spray.
2. In a medium saucepan over medium heat, bring water, milk, butter, sugar, and salt to a boil. Reduce heat to low and stir in flour. With a wooden spoon, beat vigorously for about 2 minutes, or until dough is smooth and pulls away from sides of pan.
3. Let cool for 5 minutes; transfer to medium bowl. With an electric mixer on medium speed, beat in eggs, one at a time, beating well after each addition until dough is smooth and shiny.
4. Transfer dough to a piping bag fitted with a large open tip or large star tip and pipe portions of dough in desired size onto prepared pans, keeping éclairs 2 inches apart (you can also use a Ziploc bag with a 1/2-inch cut in the corner). Bake for 15 minutes; reduce oven temperature to 375°F and bake for 12 to 15 minutes longer, or until éclairs are golden and crisp. Remove from oven and let cool completely on a wire rack.
5. Make pastry cream. In a medium saucepan over medium heat, heat milk and vanilla bean paste to just below boiling.
6. In a medium bowl whisk together sugar, cornstarch, and salt. Whisk in yolks until mixture is smooth. Gradually whisk in the hot milk until blended; return mixture to saucepan over medium heat and continue to whisk until thick. Remove from heat and whisk in butter.
7. Transfer to a medium bowl and cover surface with plastic wrap, pressing directly onto surface to prevent skin from forming. Let cool for about 15 minutes, and then refrigerate for 2 to 3 hours, or until mixture is cold.
8. Make chocolate topping. In a small saucepan over medium heat, heat milk to simmer. Put chocolate into a heatproof bowl and pour milk over; whisk until chocolate is melted and smooth.
9. To assemble, with a serrated knife, cut éclairs in half lengthwise. Transfer pastry cream to a piping bag fitted with large round tip and pipe onto bottom half of éclairs; cover with top half.
10. Spoon or brush chocolate over éclairs and transfer to a wire rack (with paper towel or parchment paper underneath to catch drips). Refrigerate until ready to serve.

Tatiana Shumbosova | Dreamstime.com

MERINGUES

Makes 12

Meringue nests with a dreamy filling of mascarpone and a topping of fresh berries are always a welcome offering on the sweets course. You can switch the fruits to take advantage of what's in season—thinly sliced peaches, plums, or pears—or switch the filling from mascarpone to lemon curd. How about a little of each?

FOR THE MERINGUES

- 3 large egg whites, at room temperature
- 3/4 cup sugar
- 1/4 tsp. cornstarch
- 1 tsp. white vinegar

FOR THE FILLING

- 1/4 cup mascarpone
- 1/4 cup heavy (whipping) cream
- Lemon curd (pg. 59 and 97), optional
- Fresh berries, for topping
- Fresh mint, for garnish

1. Make meringues. Preheat oven to 250°F. Line a baking sheet with parchment paper; outline twelve 2-inch rounds with a pencil and then turn paper over.
2. In the bowl of a stand mixer fitted with a whisk attachment, beat egg whites on high speed for 5 to 6 minutes, or until soft peaks form.
3. Gradually beat in sugar, 1 tablespoon at a time, until fully incorporated. Beat in cornstarch and vinegar; continue to beat for 8 to 10 minutes, or until stiff, shiny peaks form.
4. Transfer mixture to a piping bag fitted with a large open star tip. Starting in the center of each traced round, pipe mixture outward into 12 evenly sized rounds (with piping tip, make an indentation in center for filling). Bake for 50 to 55 minutes (do not open door); turn off oven and let meringues sit in oven for 1 to 2 hours to dry and crisp. Remove from oven and lift meringues from parchment.
5. Make filling. In a small bowl, whip mascarpone and cream with an electric mixer on medium speed until smooth. Spoon a little into the center of each meringue (or spoon in lemon curd) and top with a few berries; garnish with a sprig of mint. Unfilled meringues can be stored in an airtight container for up to a week.

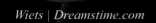
Wiets | Dreamstime.com

CHOCOLATE-ORANGE CUPCAKES WITH ORANGE CREAM CHEESE ICING

Makes 14

RICH, dark, and bold, these cupcakes combine two powerful flavors: chocolate and orange. And just when you thought cream cheese icing was reserved only for carrot cake, you'll find it to be just what's needed to balance the two flavors of this cupcake.

FOR THE CUPCAKES

- 1/2 cup cocoa powder
- 1 1/3 cups flour
- 3/4 tsp. baking soda
- 1/4 tsp. salt
- 4 oz. butter, at room temperature
- 1 cup sugar
- 2 large eggs
- 1 teaspoon orange extract
- 1/2 cup milk
- 1/2 cup hot water
- 3 tbsp. grated orange zest

FOR THE ICING

- 4 oz. butter, at room temperature
- 2 oz. butter flavor vegetable shortening, such as Crisco brand
- 1 tsp. vanilla
- 4 oz. cream cheese, at room temperature
- 2 tbsp. grated orange zest
- 6 cups confectioners' sugar
- 2 to 3 tbsp. milk

1. Make cupcakes. Preheat oven to 350°F. Line cups of a standard cupcake pan with paper liners; line another pan with 2 liners.
2. In a small bowl, sift together cocoa, flour, baking soda, and salt.
3. In a medium bowl, beat butter and sugar with an electric mixer on medium speed until light and fluffy. Beat in eggs, one at a time, beating well after each addition; beat in orange extract.
4. Beat in half the flour mixture and then beat in the milk. Beat in remaining flour and then beat in water and orange zest until combined.
5. Spoon or scoop mixture into prepared pan, filling each cup three quarters full. Bake for 15 to 17 minutes, or until a skewer inserted into center comes out clean. Remove from oven and let cool completely on a wire rack. Repeat with remaining batter.
6. Make icing. In a large bowl, beat butter and shortening with an electric mixer on medium speed until blended. Beat in vanilla, cream cheese, and orange zest for 2 to 3 minutes, or until blended. Gradually beat in confectioners' sugar, adding milk a little at a time, until smooth. Transfer to a piping bag fitted with a large open-star tip and decoratively pipe onto cupcakes. Refrigerate for 1 hour.

EARL GREY CUPCAKES WITH LEMON BUTTERCREAM ICING

Makes 12

EARL Grey is a black tea flavored with oil from the rind of a bergamot orange, a citrus fruit with the appearance and flavor somewhere between an orange and a lemon. While the tea is "quintessentially British," its unique flavor makes it popular around the world as a hot drink and as an ingredient in baking. These cupcakes use the tea twice—first with tea bags brewed in milk and again with loose tea mixed with the dry ingredients. If you need even more, you can sprinkle loose tea over the icing!

FOR THE CUPCAKES

- 1/2 cup milk
- 2 Earl Grey tea bags
- 1 1/4 cups flour
- 1 tsp. baking powder
- 1/8 tsp. salt
- 3 oz. butter, at room temperature
- 3/4 cup sugar
- 2 large eggs
- 1 tsp. vanilla extract
- 1 tsp. Earl Grey tea
- 1 tbsp. grated lemon zest

FOR THE ICING

- 4 oz. unsalted butter, at room temperature
- 2 cups confectioners' sugar
- 3 tbsp. milk
- Grated zest and juice of 1 lemon
- Pinch of salt
- Earl Grey tea, for sprinkling (optional)

1. Make cupcakes. Preheat oven to 325°F. Line cups of a standard cupcake pan with paper liners.
2. In a small saucepan over medium heat, combine milk and tea bags; heat for 2 to 3 minutes, or until warm. Remove from heat and let steep for 20 minutes; remove and discard tea bags.
3. In a medium bowl, whisk together flour, baking powder, and salt.
4. In a large bowl, beat butter and sugar with an electric mixer on medium speed until light and fluffy. Add eggs, one at a time, beating well after each addition. Beat in half the flour mixture and then beat in milk mixture. Beat in remaining flour, vanilla, tea, and lemon zest.
5. Spoon or scoop mixture into prepared pan, filling each cup two thirds full. Bake for 18 to 20 minutes, or until a skewer inserted into center comes out clean. Remove from oven and let cool completely on a wire rack.
6. Make icing. In a large bowl, beat butter with an electric mixer on medium speed for 1 minute. Beat in confectioners' sugar, milk, lemon zest, juice, and salt until smooth. Transfer to a piping bag fitted with a large open-star tip and decoratively pipe onto cupcakes. Sprinkle with tea, if desired. Refrigerate for 1 hour.

ART TEA AT THE MERRION

The most artistic take on traditional afternoon tea in all of Ireland is served in the elegant Georgian Drawing Rooms of The Merrion, one of Dublin's premier hotels. Simply called "Art Tea," the lavish repast is inspired by the hotel's own collection of nineteenth- and twentieth-century art. In-house pastry chefs create miniature sweets inspired by the works that hang throughout the hotel.

Introduced a decade ago by head chef Ed Cooney and executed by pastry chef Paul Kelly, the collection of edible art is the centrepiece of afternoon tea and is presented following the sandwiches and scones courses. In all, nine works of art have been interpreted by the chefs, each meticulously shaped and decorated by hand. The pastries, which are rotated on a weekly basis, include three from these selections:

Farm Buildings by Stephen McKenna (Hazelnut Gateau with a Coffee Bavarois); *Frying Pan, Funnel, Eggs & Lemons* by William Scott (Vanilla Biscuit with Orange Curd); *Futile Defence (Fabricated Evidence)* by John Boyd (Raspberry & Passionfruit Tart); *Shut Eye with Acolyte (Praxis)* by John Boyd (Tear Drop of Pistachio and White Chocolate Mousse); *Roses and Temple* by Patrick Hennessy (Rosewater and Orange Mousse on a White Chocolate Feuilletine); *Self Portrait 1912* by Suarin Elizabeth Leech (Lime Sponge, Orange Chiboust & Lemon Jelly Curd); *The Old Fox* by John Doherty (Green Apple Macaroon); *Path Moorea* by Pauline Bewick (Chocolate Trinity); and *Madonna and Child* by Mainie Jellet (Passionfruit and Orange Cheesecake).

The Merrion Hotel

Kuvona | Dreamstime.com

MINCEMEAT

Makes 2 cups

IN Ireland, from mid–November to the end of the year all thoughts turn to Christmas and that includes holiday offerings on afternoon tea menus: the most popular, gingerbread, fruit cakes, and pies and tarts made with mincemeat, a mixture of chopped dried fruits, spices, and spirits. Mincemeat was developed more than 500 years ago in England as a way of preserving meat without salting or smoking and was esteemed as holiday fare there during the era of Henry VII (1457–1509), who proclaimed Christmas a day of feasting. Some early recipes for mincemeat used suet, veal or mutton, and gradually cooks added ingredients like apples, Seville oranges, and red wine. When there was no longer any need to preserve meat with honey or spices, the meat in mincemeat was eliminated and replaced with fruit alone, although some cooks still use a bit of suet in their recipes.

In Elizabethan England, huge mince pies were made during the twelve days of Christmas, and it became customary to offer a slice to visiting guests. The leap from England to Ireland was a short one, and mincemeat soon became a favorite ingredient in an Irish Christmas as well, especially in the form of mince pies, tarts, and muffins. Along with steamed pudding and fruitcake, mincemeat has been the standard-bearer of traditional Christmas desserts for centuries and a popular addition to holiday teatime in Ireland. You can purchase jars of mincemeat, some with brandy or rum, or try your hand at this homemade version.

- 1/4 cup sultanas (golden raisins)
- 1/4 cup currants
- 1/4 cup raisins
- 1/4 cup candied mixed peel, chopped
- 2 tbsp. chopped candied cherries
- Grated zest and juice of 1 lemon
- Grated zest of 1 orange
- 1 Granny Smith apple, cored and shredded
- 1/4 cup (packed) dark brown sugar
- 2 tsp. pumpkin pie spice or Mixed Spice (pg. 61)
- 2 tbsp. fresh white breadcrumbs
- 3 tbsp. brandy
- 2 tbsp. dark rum

1. Combine all ingredients in a large bowl, cover, and leave at room temperature for at least 24 hours. Transfer to a glass container, stir in additional brandy or rum, if desired, cover, and refrigerate for up to 2 weeks.

Foods of Athenry

MINCEMEAT TARTS

Makes 18

These star-studded tarts are a "must" for Christmas tea. You can buy packages of them in shops everywhere in Ireland, but the best ones, of course, are the ones you make at home.

FOR THE PASTRY

- 2 cups all-purpose flour
- 1/2 cup ground almonds
- 5 oz. cold butter, cut into pieces
- Grated zest of 1 orange
- 4 tbsp. sugar
- 1 large egg yolk
- 1 tbsp. ice water

FOR THE FILLING

- 1 cup homemade or prepared mincemeat
- 1 large egg white, beaten
- Confectioners' sugar, for dusting

1. Make pastry. In a food processor, combine flour, almonds, butter, zest, and sugar. Pulse 8 to 10 times, or until mixture resembles coarse crumbs. Add egg yolk and water; process for 10 to 20 seconds, or until dough comes together.
2. Dust a work surface with flour. Turn out dough, form it into a ball, and then flatten into a disk; cover with plastic wrap and refrigerate for 30 minutes.
3. Preheat oven to 375°F. On a floured surface, roll out dough to a 1/8-inch-thick round. With a 4-inch cookie cutter, cut out 18 rounds; transfer rounds into cups of 2 standard tart pans. Reroll pastry scraps, and with a star-shaped cookie cutter, cut out 18 small stars.
4. Spoon mincemeat into shells and top each with a star. Brush pastry stars and tart edges with the egg white and bake for 20 to 22 minutes, or until pastry is golden and filling is bubbling. Remove from oven and transfer to a wire rack to let cool for about 10 minutes. Sprinkle with confectioners' sugar before serving.

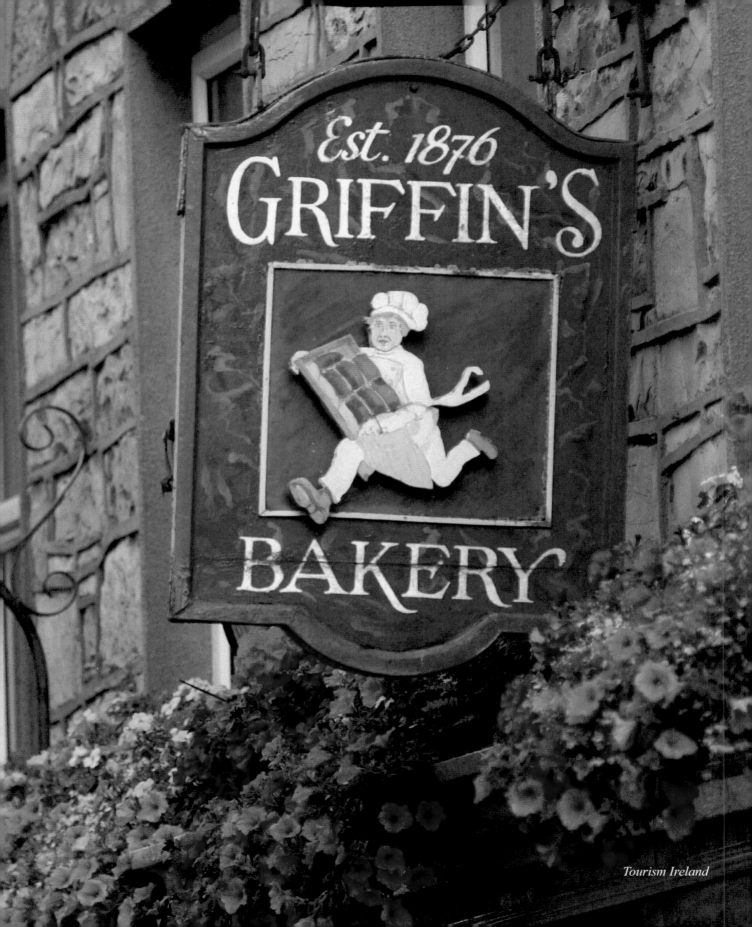

Est. 1876
GRIFFIN'S

BAKERY

Tourism Ireland

SHORTBREAD MINCE PIES

Makes 24

THIS recipe, from Griffin's Bakery on Shop Street, Galway, is a Christmas specialty. There the pies are made with shortbread cookies rather than pastry and are filled with homemade whiskey-flavored mincemeat. The shortbread crust adds a touch of sweetness to the little pies and the added whiskey, well, an extra touch of Christmas!

FOR THE SHORTBREAD

- 3 cups all-purpose flour
- 1/2 cup sugar
- 8 oz. cold butter, cut into pieces
- 1 large egg yolk
- 5 to 8 tbsp. ice water

FOR THE FILLING

- 1 1/4 cups prepared or homemade mincemeat
- 2 tbsp. Irish whiskey
- Confectioners' sugar, for dusting

1. Make shortbread. In a food processor, combine flour, sugar, and butter. Pulse 8 to 10 times, or until mixture resembles coarse crumbs. Add egg yolk and water; process for 10 to 20 seconds, or until dough comes together. Gather dough and form it into a ball; cover with plastic wrap and refrigerate for 1 hour.
2. Preheat oven to 325°F. Line a baking sheet with parchment paper.
3. Dust a work surface with flour. Cut dough in half; roll out each half to a 1/4-inch-thick round. With a 2 1/2-inch cookie cutter, cut out 24 rounds from each half. Place half on the prepared baking sheet, spacing 1 inch apart.
4. Make filling. In a small bowl, combine mincemeat and whiskey. Spoon 1 teaspoon into center of each pastry round; cover with a plain pastry round. Press edges with a fork to seal, and then brush with a little water; pierce tops with a fork.
5. Bake pies for about 25 minutes, or until lightly browned. Remove from oven and then transfer pies to a wire rack to cool. Repeat with remaining dough and filling. Dust cooled pies with confectioners' sugar before serving.

Wade Murphy

APPLE-DATE STICKY TOFFEE PUDDING CAKES

Makes 24

THESE little cakes, reminiscent of sticky toffee pudding, are perfect for teatime. In addition to the dates and nuts usually found in the popular pudding, the grated apples add a holiday touch. The recipe, from Wade Murphy, chef-proprietor of 1826 Adare, a lovely restaurant in the charming Limerick village, can be made a day or two ahead; leave the cakes at room temperature and reheat the sauce in a microwave.

FOR THE PUDDINGS

- 1 1/4 cups chopped dates
- 1 1/4 cups water
- 1 1/2 tsp. baking soda
- 4 oz. butter, at room temperature
- 1 1/4 cups sugar
- 3 large eggs
- 2 1/2 cups flour
- 2 cooking apples, peeled, cored, and grated

FOR THE TOFFEE SAUCE

- 1/4 cup water
- 3/4 cups sugar
- 4 oz. butter, cut into pieces
- 2/3 cup heavy (whipping) cream

1. Make puddings. In a medium saucepan, combine water, dates, and soda. Bring to a boil, stir once or twice, and then remove from heat and let cool completely.
2. Preheat oven to 325° F. Coat the cups of two standard cupcake pans with nonstick spray.
3. In a medium bowl, beat butter and sugar with an electric mixer on medium speed until light and fluffy. Beat in eggs, one at a time, and then fold in flour, date mixture, and apples. Spoon batter into prepared pans and bake for 25 minutes, or until a skewer inserted into center comes out clean. Remove from oven and let cool on a wire rack for 10 minutes.
4. Make sauce. In a medium saucepan over medium heat, bring water and sugar to a boil. Cook for 3 to 5 minutes, or until mixture begins to caramelize. Whisk in butter until blended; whisk in cream until smooth. To serve, spoon warm toffee sauce over warm puddings.

Marcinjucha | Dreamstime.com

IRISH WHISKEY CAKE

Serves 10 to 12

WHISKEY cake with candied fruits is popular at Christmas and for special occasions like weddings and christenings. This recipe is much lighter and more like a spicy raisin cake than a heavy fruitcake, so it often appears on a holiday teatime menu. It can be served with the whiskey-flavored icing or with a simple dusting of confectioners' sugar.

FOR THE CAKE

- 1 cup sultanas (golden raisins)
- 1 1/2 cups water
- 1 1/2 cups all-purpose flour
- 2 tsp. baking powder
- 1 tsp. baking soda
- 3/4 tsp. ground cloves
- 3/4 tsp. nutmeg
- Dash of ground allspice
- 1/2 tsp. salt
- 4 oz. butter, at room temperature
- 1/2 cup sugar
- 1 large egg
- 1 cup chopped walnuts
- 1/4 cup Irish whiskey

FOR THE ICING

- 6 oz. butter, at room temperature
- 3 cups confectioners' sugar
- 1 tbsp. milk
- 1/4 cup Irish whiskey
- Chopped walnuts, for garnish (optional)

1. Make cake. Preheat oven to 350° F. Butter a 9-inch springform pan and dust with flour; tap out excess.
2. In a small saucepan over medium heat, bring raisins and water to a boil. Reduce heat to medium-low and simmer for 20 minutes, or until liquid begins to thicken. Drain, reserving 3/4 cup of liquid; set aside to cool.
3. In a medium bowl, sift together flour, baking powder, baking soda, cloves, nutmeg, allspice, and salt.
4. In a large bowl, beat butter and sugar with an electric mixer on medium speed until light and fluffy; add egg and beat until smooth. Fold in flour mixture alternately with reserved liquid; stir in raisins, walnuts, and whiskey.
5. Transfer to prepared pan and bake for 30 to 35 minutes, or until a skewer inserted into center comes out clean. Remove from oven and let cool on a wire rack for 15 minutes. Release sides of pan, invert cake, and remove wax paper. Return cake to upright and let cool completely.
6. Make icing. In a large bowl, beat butter and sugar with an electric mixer on medium speed until smooth. Add milk and whiskey; beat until smooth. With an offset spatula, spread icing over top and sides of cake; garnish with walnut halves, if desired. Let icing set for 15 to 20 minutes before cutting cake into slices.

NICHOLAS MOSSE POTTERY, *Margaret M. Johnson*

INDEX

FOR MORE INFORMATION ABOUT
Margaret M. Johnson
&
Teatime in Ireland
please visit:

www.irishcook.com
www.facebook.com/IrishCookbook

....

For more information about
AMBASSADOR INTERNATIONAL
please visit:

www.ambassador-international.com
@AmbassadorIntl
www.facebook.com/AmbassadorIntl